アメリカ不動産投資の実態。

金井規雄

在米40年の元バンカーが
多数の成功事例を元に実証！

プラチナ出版

ビバリーヒルズのコンドミニアムのバックヤード＆リビング
1927年に建てられた物件です。

after

Before

リビング・キッチン（実例3：158ページ）

after

Before

タウンハウスのバスルームをリフォーム（実例4：161ページ）

まえがき

不動産の基本・根本は人口（＝需要）ですが、日本はすでに人口減少時代に入っており、しかも減少しているのは若者、とくに産業労働者人口で、逆に増えているのは高齢者です。全体的に人口が減少しているなかで高齢者が増えているので、いわゆる"超高齢化社会"に進んでいます。世界でも類を見ない速さでどんどん突き進んでいます。

さらに、2020年の東京オリンピック後、2022年の生産緑地化の解放、2025年からは団塊世代が75歳以上の後期高齢者になり相続が一気に増えることなどから、土地・不動産暴落が起こると予測されています。実際にはすでに起こり始めており、事態はどんどん悪化していくそうです。また、所有者不明の土地は全体の20％を占めるほどに増えています。もちろん、この予測が必ず的中する保証はありませんが、不動産の原理・原則となる需要の人口が減少しており、土地などの供給が過剰となる可能性が高いとなれば、確実に不動産価値（＝価格）は下落していくことになります。

また、これらの動きのなかで、不動産の価値が今後、維持もしくは上昇するのは、全体の10％から20％ぐらいまでと、不動産コンサルタントや専門家が予測しています。つまり、80％から90％は価値が減少、またはなくなるということですが、こちらも当たるかどうかわかりません。

しかしながら、予測が外れるとしても兆候は悪くなるばかりで、影響がそれほど大きくなくても、今後不動産市況が良くなったり、改善したりする可能性はかなり低いとみるべきでしょう。全体的に悪くなっていくのが大方の予想ではないでしょうか？　人口は減少していくのですから、不動産の需要も減ることになり、市況が改善し良くなることは困難なのが現状です。

このような状況において、海外不動産も視野に入れ、資産防衛のみならず投資リスクを最小限に留め、自身の資産安定・向上を図るべきです。では、どこの海外不動産が最適なのでしょうか？　ズバリ、それはアメリカの不動産です。4ページの人口に関するグラフをご覧ください。アメリカの人口は1950年が1億6000万人、2015年が3億2000万人で、2100年には4億5000万人に達する見込みです。先進国の中

まえがき

で、人口の増加が鮮明なのは、アメリカです。

アメリカの不動産が最適である主な理由は、次の7つがあげられます。

1 外国人でも不動産が所有できる。
2 契約などが法治国家で明確である。
3 所有権が明確で安心できる。
4 空室リスクがない。
5 価値が上昇する。
6 耐久性が高い。
7 節税効果が高い。

それぞれの項目については、本文中で詳細に解説いたします。

アメリカの不動産であれば何でもいい、どこでもいいということではありません。本文でも解説いたしますが、節税に適していることからも、とくに西海岸の不動産が最適です。

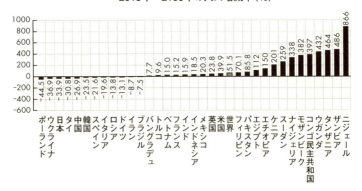

（注）中位推計の結果　（資料）国連、World Population Prospects: The 2017 Revision

■世界と主要国の将来人口推計

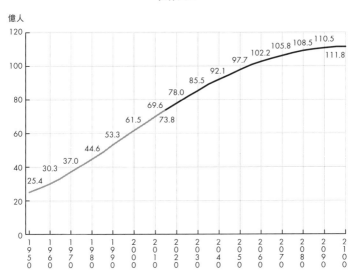

世界人口

なかでもロサンゼルスは不動産物件の取扱件数が一番多い市場ですので、ロサンゼルスを中心に検討されるのが賢明といえます。

本書では、アメリカ不動産投資で見過ごすことができない実践的で大事な点、空室リスクや訴訟、保険、所有権などをくわしく解説いたします。

目次

まえがき 1

序章 アメリカ不動産がベスト

1 アメリカの国力 14
①経済（＝GDP）＋金融 15／②軍事力 16／③人口 17／④学術・研究力 18

2 アメリカ不動産の最適性 20

3 アメリカ不動産の魅力 22
①収益性 22／②資産価値が高い 26／③節税 26

第1章 ロケーションがすべて

1 アメリカをロケーションの区別でエリア分けしてみる

①「＋A」ロケーション 37 ／②「A」ロケーション 37 ／③「ーA」ロケーション 38 ／④「＋B」ロケーション 38 ／⑤「B」ロケーション 38

2 各エリアのロケーション

①サンタモニカ 40 ／②ビバリーヒルズ 40 ／③ウエスト・ハリウッド 40 ／④ウエスト・ロサンゼルス 41 ／⑤ベニス 42 ／⑥カルバーシティ 41 ／⑦マリナ・デル・レイ 42 ／⑧トーランス 43 ／⑨パロスバーデス 43 ／⑩マンハッタンビーチ 44 ／⑪ハモサビーチ 44 ／⑫レドンドビーチ 44 ／⑬グレンデール 44 ／⑭パサデナ 45 ／⑮バーバンク 45 ／⑯スタジオシティ 45 ／⑰ノースハリウッド 45 ／⑱バレンシア 46 ／⑲ロングビーチ 46 ／⑳ハンティントンビーチ 46 ／㉑ニューポートビーチ 47 ／㉒アーバイン 47 ／㉓コスタメサ 47

こぼれ話1　ニューマネー 50

第2章 アメリカ不動産の空室リスク

1 空率リスクはない 58
2 テナント属性 65
こぼれ話2 グローバル・バンクHSBC 68

第3章 アメリカ不動産と訴訟

1 訴訟 72
①テナント希望者のスクリーニング 73／②賃貸借契約書 74／③保険 75

第4章 アメリカ不動産の建物に対する考え方

1 土地より建物比率が高いアメリカ不動産 100

2 長い耐久年数 108

こぼれ話4 ブランド志向の日本 113

2 保険について 91
① 火災保険 92 ／ ② 損害賠償保険とオーナー保険（HO6） 92 ／ ③ 地震保険 95 ／ ④ 賃貸者（テナント）保険 95

こぼれ話3 人口減少 97

第5章 所有権

1 譲渡証書 116

2 タイトル・レポート 124

こぼれ話5 ブームは終わりの始まり？ 133

第6章 改装（リフォーム）

1 レントコントロール 136

2 家賃相場 139

実例1 150／実例2 156／実例3 158／実例4 161

こぼれ話6 老後の資金 163

第7章 売買取引と契約書

1 買付けオファーから合意に至るまで 168
2 エスクロー 198
3 不動産手数料 207

補章 物件・案件の紹介

あとがき 239

装丁・DTP◎二ノ宮 匡（ニクスインク）
地図◎川田あきひこ

序章 アメリカ不動産がベスト

1 アメリカの国力

日本以外の世界の国々の中で、どこに不動産投資をするべきかを考えるとき、安全性、安定性、そして成長性がそろっている国が最適だと考えられますので、やはり先進国ということになります。将来の値上がりを期待する成長性だけでみると、東南アジアの国々も検討できますが、安全性と安定性を考慮しますと、難しい面があります。

先進国の中で考えますと、ヨーロッパ、カナダ、オーストラリアなどが出てきますが、では、その先進国の海外不動産のなかでも、なぜアメリカの不動産が一番なのか？ それは、国力が世界で一番であることが大きな理由です。国力が一番であるということは、次の経済力・金融、軍事力、学術などあらゆる面で秀でているということで、その国の不動産は、世界でトップレベルということになります。それでは、国力とは何かといえば、次の4つが主なファクターかと思います。

① 経済力（＝GDP）＋金融
② 軍事力
③ 人口
④ 学術・研究力

① 経済（＝GDP）＋金融

図表0-1をご覧ください。2016年度の国別GDPです。アメリカは18・6兆ドルのGDPですが、一方、中国が11・2兆ドル、日本が4・9兆ドルです。中国と日本を足してもアメリカには及ばないのです。イギリスかフランスを足さないとアメリカには比肩しません。いかにアメリカの経済力が大きいかがわかります。

世界の名だたる企業も、ほぼ全分野においてアメリカの企業がトップに名を連ねています（**図表0-2参照**）。ボーイング、グーグル、アップル、インテル、デュポン、GE、ジョンソン&ジョンソン、プロクター&ギャンブル、コカコーラなど。

それから、世界の基軸通貨はドルです。そのドルの金融政策の決定や通貨発行権を有するのがFRB（連邦準備制度理事会）で、FRBのオーナーはJPモルガンチェイス銀行、

図表 0-1　2016年度国別GDP（単位：百万ドル）

	国名	GDP
1	アメリカ	18,624,450
2	中国	11,232,108
3	日本	4,936,543
4	ドイツ	3,479,232
5	イギリス	2,629,188
6	フランス	2,466,472
7	インド	2,263,792
8	イタリア	1,850,735
9	ブラジル	1,798,622
10	カナダ	1,529,760

ゴールドマンサックス、ロスチャイルド銀行などで、私企業になります。多くの方がFRBのことをアメリカ政府の中央銀行と思っていますが、一私企業なのです。オーナー企業をみますと、ユダヤ系色が強いというより、ユダヤ系そのものです。

最も留意すべき点は、FRBは金利基準を決定できるだけではなく、ドルの発行権を有していることです。つまり、ドル紙幣をいくらでも彼らの思い通りに刷れるということなのです。詳細は、自著「ドル資産を持て！」（週刊住宅新聞社刊）をご参照ください。

②軍事力

アメリカは、軍事力でも世界ナンバーワ

ンです。

単純に武器保有量や保有できる容積だけではなく、技術力も世界ナンバーワンといえるでしょう。掃除機のルンバは偵察機が原型であり、戦闘前線に送る武器弾薬や食料は大型ロボットで賄えるようです。

③人口

人口においては、アメリカは中国、インドに続きますが、最も重要な点は、次の2点です。

1　総人口が今後も増えていくのは、先進国の中ではアメリカだけであること（イギリスも今後、少しだけ増えるようですが、その影響は限定的と思われています）。

2　アメリカのミレニアル世代が総人口の多くを占めるようになり、産業人口がどんどん増え、さらなる景気上昇が見込まれること。したがって、不動産価格も上昇することです。

＊2000年代に成人または社会人の世代で、1980年代から2000年代初頭に生まれた世代のことをいいます。ベビーブーマー（団塊世代）と同等かそれ以上の人口で、2025年にはアメリカの総人口の70～75％を占めるといわれています。
このミレニアル世代の人口増加が不動産市況をさらに堅調に推移させることになるのですが、詳細は後述の「アメリカ不動産の見通し」で述べたいと思います。

④ 学術・研究力

②の軍事力でも述べましたが、世界ナンバーワンの技術力、学術が軍事力の増強から宇宙開発に至るまでの幅広い分野をカバーし、国力を支えます。

実は、筆者の考えるアメリカの世界ナンバーワンたるゆえん、根底は、教育だと考えています。アメリカの教育で特筆すべきは、個人の能力を引き出し、個人の特長を尊重する点です。要するに、全く新しい考えややりかたを尊重するのです。

そもそも飛行機、電気、電話、コンピューター、スマホなど社会に革新的な物品やシステムを産出してきたのはアメリカです。筆者は、これは教育の賜物と考えております。また、奨学金制度が公私ともども充実していることです。ほとんどの大学には、100前後の奨学金プログラムがあります。

以上のことから、アメリカの不動産に投資することは安全で安心といえるとともに将来性も見込め、資産価値の上昇につながります。

序章
アメリカ不動産がベスト

図表 0-2 世界のトップ企業ランキング（時価総額ベース）（2017年11月末現在）

	前月比	企業名	$10億	国名
1	⇒	アップル	882.3315	アメリカ
2	⇒	アルファベット	714.7747	アメリカ
3	⇒	マイクロソフト	649.3370	アメリカ
4	⇒	アマゾン・ドット・コム	567.0430	アメリカ
5	⇒	フェイスブック	514.8511	アメリカ
6	↑	テンセント・ホールディング	479.9301	中国
7	⇒	バークシャー・ハサウェイ	477.6869	アメリカ
8	↓	アリババ・グループ・ホールディング	447.8998	中国
9	⇒	ジョンソン＆ジョンソン	374.3128	アメリカ
10	⇒	JPモルガン・チェース	362.6557	アメリカ
11	⇒	エクソン・モービル	352.9085	アメリカ
12	⇒	中国工商銀行	321.3251	中国
13	⇒	サムスン電子	320.7071	韓国
14	⇒	バンク・オブ・アメリカ	293.8303	アメリカ
15	↑	ウォルマート・ストアーズ	290.4456	アメリカ
16	↓	ウェルズ・ファーゴ	278.0730	アメリカ
17	↓	中国建設銀行	276.3173	中国
18	↑	ネスレ	274.0966	スイス
19	↓	ロイヤル・ダッチ・シェル	264.5423	オランダ
20	↑	ビザ	233.2462	アメリカ
21	↑	P&G	228.3008	アメリカ
22	⇒	ペトロチャイナ	226.8243	中国
23	⇒	シェブロン	226.0065	アメリカ
24	↓	アンハイザー・ブッシュ・インベブ	225.6589	ベルギー
25	↑	AT&T	223.3370	アメリカ
26	↑	ユナイテッドヘルス・グループ	221.1121	アメリカ
27	↑	ファイザー	216.1352	アメリカ
28	↑	ロシュ・ホールディング	215.3174	スイス
29	↑	中国平安保険	214.0727	中国
30	↓	台湾・セミコンダクター・マニュファクチャリング	213.8400	台湾

出典：GFP

2 アメリカ不動産の最適性

まえがきにも書きましたが、アメリカの不動産が最適である7つの理由をあげました。

1 外国人でも不動産が所有できる。
2 契約などが法治国家で明確である。
3 所有権が明確で安心できる。
4 空室リスクがない。
5 価値が上昇する。
6 耐久性が高い。
7 節税効果が高い。

これだけの利点があるのは、アメリカ不動産だけといっても過言ではないと思います。

序章
アメリカ不動産がベスト

図表 0-3 **世界の外貨準備に占める各通貨の割合（2015年6月末時点）**

アメリカドル	63.8%
ユーロ	20.5%
ポンド	4.7%
日本円	3.8%
カナダドル	1.9%
オーストラリアドル	1.9%

出典：国際通貨基金（IMF）

 特に「1」の非居住者である外国人でも、不動産の所有権を認めております。自国民であろうと外国人であろうと、平等に所有権を認めているのです。外国人でも、これほど寛大で正々堂々と不動産投資ができるのはアメリカならではでしょう。

 一番大事な所有権につきましては、「第5章 所有権」でくわしく述べたいと思います。アメリカと日本では不動産の登記について全く違う形式ですので、これをしっかり理解していただきたいと思います。

3 アメリカ不動産の魅力

アメリカ不動産の魅力は、次の3つがあげられます。

① **安定した収益性**
② **高い資産価値**
③ **節税**

① 収益性

第2章で解説しますが、空室リスクがないために収入が安定し、また家賃値上げや強制退去も可能ですので、しっかりとした収益が見込めます。家賃は通常、毎年値上げできますので、数年で当初より高い利回が達成できます。

序章
アメリカ不動産がベスト

図表 0-4 世界の軍事力トップ10

1	アメリカ
2	ロシア
3	中国
4	インド
5	フランス
6	イギリス
7	日本
8	トルコ
9	ドイツ
10	エジプト

出典:米国の軍事力分析機関グローバル・ファイヤーパワー(GFP)

図表 0-5 ロサンゼルス不動産価格推移表

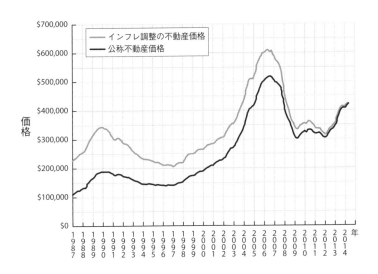

所得税など総合課税される収入については、超過累進課税されるため、最大45％となります（2015年分以降）。さらに2037年までは、所得税額の2.1％の復興特別所得税が上乗せされるため、実質45.945％となり、ここに住民税が一律10％課税され、トータル55.945％もの税金を納めなければなりません。一方、長期譲渡所得として課税された場合、税率は20.315％となり、30.525％もの節税が実現することとなります。

毎年の所得税
559万円×4年
＝**2,236**万円

55.945％

30.525％

20.3145％

節税分
1,423.4万円

譲渡所得税
812万円

■毎年の所得税：2015年分以降

課税される所得金額	税率	控除額
195万円以下	5％	0円
195万円を超え330万円以下	10％	97,500円
330万円を超え695万円以下	20％	427,500円
695万円を超え900万円以下	23％	636,000円
900万円を超え1,800万円以下	33％	1,536,000円
1,800万円を超え4,000万円以下	40％	2,796,000円
4,000万円超	45％	4,796,000円

税率＝所得税率×復興特別所得税2.1％＋住民税10％
＊最大55.945％

■売却時の税金

	短期譲渡所得	長期譲渡所得
所得税	30％	15％
復興特別所得税	0.63％	0.315％
住民税	9％	5％
トータル	39.63％	20.315％

序章
アメリカ不動産がベスト

図表 0-6 節税シミュレーション

■ 節税シミュレーション[保有時]

[想定条件]
価格5,000万円／建物割合80％／償却期間4年の物件に投資した場合。
毎年の減価償却費＝5,000万円×80％÷4＝1,000万円(損金計上)

投資前		投資後		節税額
課税所得	税額(所・住)	課税所得	税額(所・住)	280万円
1,000万円	280万円	0万円	0万円	451万円
2,000万円	731万円	1,000万円	280万円	508万円
3,000万円	1,240万円	2,000万円	731万円	508万円
4,000万円	1,748万円	3,000万円	1,240万円	559万円
5,000万円	2,308万円	4,000万円	1,748万円	559万円
6,000万円	2,867万円	5,000万円	2,308万円	559万円
7,000万円	3,426万円	6,000万円	2,867万円	559万円
10,0000万円	5,105万円	9,000万円	4,545万円	559万円

価格5,000万円の不動産を購入した場合、4年合計2,236万円＋家賃収入を獲得。
4年間の節税額は毎年559万円となります。
＊不動産の賃料および減価償却以外の必要経費、不動産購入手数料は考慮しない。

■ 節税シミュレーション[売却時]

購入時と同額の5,000万円で不動産を売却した場合、5年間保有することで
最終的に節税額は1,423.4万円となります。

・インフレを加味せず、購入時と同額(5,000万円)で売却した場合の税金

売却価格5,000万円－残存簿価1,000万円＝4,000万円(課税価格)
4,000万円×税率20.315％(長期譲渡)＝812.6万円(売却時の税金)

・トータルの節税額

559万円×4年－812.6万円＝1,423.4万円
5年超保有することで、最終的に1,423.4万円を節税することに。

② 資産価値が高い

ロケーションの良いところの物件は、資産価値の下振れの影響が限定的である一方、上昇の度合いが大きいので、価値の安定につながり、上昇の速度も速くなります。リーマンショック後の不動産価格の急落で、次章で述べますロケーションの低いCクラスで70～90％の下落、中間のBクラスで30～70％の下落でしたが、Aクラスのロケーションの物件は、10～30％程度の下落に留まりました。

筆者のお客様が、Aクラスのロケーションのマンハッタンビーチの3戸もの物件を2009年9月に194万ドルで購入しました。CAPは4％でしたが、現在のCAPは5.7％に上昇し、現在の価値は400万ドル以上です。

③ 節税

例の木造築22年以上の物件は、4年間の加速度償却が可能な物件です。加速度償却とは、決算上の赤字を所得収入に合算して課税対象所得を圧縮することにより、税金を大幅に減少させる方法です。筆者もこの5年間で50数件以上の節税目的の物件のお世話をしてきました。最近では、2016年の10月後半に会計検査院が、2018年1月には国税庁がこの海外中古不動産利用の節税について対策を検討し、節税スキームに待ったをかける指摘

をしました。この流れの中で、近い将来、海外中古不動産を利用した節税が規制されるはずですが、償却が取れなくなるというわけではなく、償却年数が長くなるなどその度合いが緩くなるという程度でしょう。加速度償却は4年間ですが、売却は5年後にすることがベストな出口戦略です。理由は、5年以上であれば長期保有ということで、分離課税で約半分の税率になるからです。

さらに、節税はこの償却だけではないのです。アメリカ不動産を所有することによって、アメリカの納税者番号を取得しアメリカの生命保険を手当てすることで、大胆な相続税対策ができるのです。今、仮に1億円の現預金があるとします。万一のことがあれば、相続税は約半分の50％が課せられ、残るのは半分、つまり5000万円です。ところが、この1億円でアメリカの生命保険を購入しますと、年齢や健康状態にもよりますが、約4倍の死亡保障の保険になりますので、4億円の保険金が下ります。約50％の2億円が相続税で、残りの2億円が手元に残ります。残るのが5000万円がいいのか、2億円がいいのか、答えは明白ですね。

単位:USドル

1年目	2年目	3年目	4年目	5年目	6年目	合計
筑42年	筑43年	筑44年	筑45年	筑46年	筑47年	
100.0%	100.0%	100.0%	100.0%	100.0%	100.0%	
644,731	644,731	644,731	644,731	644,731	644,731	
34,800	34,800	34,800	34,800	34,800	34,800	208,800
34,800	34,800	34,800	34,800	34,800	34,800	
34,800	34,800	34,800	34,800	34,800	34,800	
14,505	14,505	14,505	14,505	14,505	14,505	87,031
2,100	2,100	2,100	2,100	2,100	2,100	
7,725	7,725	7,725	7,725	7,725	7,725	
480	480	480	480	480	480	
3,600	3,600	3,600	3,600	3,600	3,600	
600	600	600	600	600	600	
20,295	20,295	20,295	20,295	20,295	20,295	121,769
103,515	103,515	103,515	103,515			414,060
-83,220	-83,220	-83,220	-83,220	20,295	20,295	
-83,220	-83,220	-83,220	-83,220	20,295	20,295	
-239.1%	-239.1%	-239.1%	-239.1%	58.3%	58.3%	
-45,771	-45,771	-45,771	-45,771	11,162	11,162	-160,162
-37,449	-37,449	-37,449	-37,449	9,133	9,133	

-578,665	66,066	66,066	66,066	9,133	9,133	
-578,665	-512,599	-446,533	-380,468	-371,335	-362,202	

1年目	2年目	3年目	4年目	5年目	6年目	
618,000	618,000	618,000	618,000	618,000	618,000	
514,485	410,970	307,455	203,940	203,940	203,940	
68,109	68,109	68,109	68,109	68,109	68,109	
35,406	138,921	242,436	345,951	345,951	345,951	
5.7%	22.5%	39.2%	56.0%	56.0%	56.0%	
13,808	54,179	94,550	134,921	134,921	69,190	
21,598	84,742	147,886	211,030	211,030	276,761	
536,083	495,712	455,341	414,970	414,970	480,701	
-42,583	-16,888	8,808	34,503	43,635	118,499	

序章
アメリカ不動産がベスト

図表 0-7 収支シミュレーション

■ 物件名

[物件概要]

物件価格	$618,000
建物割合	67.0%
償却期間	4年
構造	木造
竣工	1974年
総戸数	1戸
物件単価	$498／sq ft
平均賃料単価	$2.3／sq ft

[投資効果]

表面利回り	5.6%
NOI利回り	3.2%

[節税効果]

初年度の損益通算額	$83,220
4年間の累計節税額	$183,084
売却後のキャッシュフロー	$118,499
CCR	18.4%

※CCR キャッシュ オン キャッシュリターン
初期投資金額(自己資金)に対する最終のCFの割合。

[資金計画]

借入額	$0
借入比率	0%
金利	4.000%
融資期間	30年間
取得諸経費	$26,731
自己資金	$618,000
初期投資金額	$644,731

[取得諸費用内訳]

タイトルインシュランス	$0	
エスクロー費用	$2,472	
コンサルティングフィ	$20,023	
ローン手数料	$0	
建物調査費用	$1,236	
管理組合費用	$0	
鑑定評価	$3,000	
取得経費合計	$26,731	4.3%

キャッシュフロー表		
経過年数		
稼働率		
投下自己資金		
収入	A	
	賃料（共益費）	
	駐車場代	
	その他収入	
売上総利益（粗利）	A	
支出	B	
	BMフィ	
	PMフィ	
	固都税	
	保険料	
	コモンチャージ	
	修繕費	
	水道光熱費	
	その他経費	
年間収支（NOI）	C=A-B	
償却	減価償却費（躯体）	D
	減価償却費（設備）	
営業利益	※1	E=C-D
営業外費用	支払利息	F
経常利益		G=E-F
	利益率	H=G/A
55%	所得税・住民税 ※2	A=G*55%
税引後利益		J=G-I

[返済計画]

借入金額残高（期首）	K
元本返済額	L
利息返済額	M
元利金返済計	N=L+M
DSCR	
年間CF（税引後）	O=J+D-L
累計CF	P=O+累積O

転売収支表（売却時）	
売却価格	Q
簿価（期末）※取得価格－減価償却	R
売却諸経費	S
経常利益	T=Q-S-R
経常利益率	U=T/Q
所得税・住民税	V=T*39/20%
税引後利益	WT-V
転売CF（税引後）	X=Q-S-(K-L)-V
トータルCF	Y=P+X-自己資金

図表 0-8　海外中古物件の節税策　富裕層に広がる

By 公認会計士・税理士　高鳥 拓也　｜　2016 年 11 月 3 日

建物の資産価値が下がりにくい海外の中古物件を利用した節税策が富裕層の間で広がっていることが、会計検査院の調べでわかりました。税の専門家は、行き過ぎた税逃れにつながるおそれがあるとして、対策の必要性を指摘しています。

会計検査院が平成 25 年の税務申告で海外に不動産を所有していた 331 人の高所得者を調べたところ、287 人が減価償却費を計上していたということです。中には節税効果が高くなる償却までの期間が短い物件の購入を繰り返している人も確認されたということです。

会計検査院は、古い中古物件の資産価値が国内外で大きく異なることを踏まえて、より公平性を高めるような減価償却費の在り方を検討する必要があるとしています。

出所：NHK NEWS WEB（2016 年 10 月 28 日）

第1章 ロケーションがすべて

1 アメリカをロケーションの区別でエリア分けしてみる

日本でも物件のロケーション（＝場所）は重要なキーポイントですが、アメリカでは絶対的な決め手となります。日本では、「へんぴで不便」「駅から遠い」などの立地が物件の価値が上がらない要因となりますが、アメリカでは、エリアによっては薬事法違反がまかり通っていたり、ギャングがいたりするなどの治安問題があり、それらのことが決定的なマイナス要因となっています。治安の良し悪し、そして生命にかかわる点が日本とは違っており、全くと言っていいほど問題の次元が違うのです。

また、アメリカの市・区域の学校制度は公立が中心です。当然ながら、親は自分の子どもにより良い学校教育を受けさせたいため、少しでも良い学校に通わせようとします。つまり、優良な学校に自分の子どもを通わせる目的で、そのような学校のある市や街に移り住みます。結果、優良学校地域の物件は、高額になります。良い学校のある区域が優良エリアになり、自然と不動産物件の価値・価格は高くなります。アメリカ人の不動産エージェ

第1章
ロケーションがすべて

図表 1-1 ロケーション水準表

ランク	内容	空室率	利回り(CAP)	該当する市
A⁺	誰もがあこがれる最高のエリア ほとんどが1軒家で、アパートの集合住宅はまずない。 Duplex(2戸)Triplex(3戸)ぐらいか。	0%～0.5%	1%～2%	ビバリーヒルズ、マンハッタンビーチなど。
A	人気の優良エリアで、最高の環境を提供。高い家賃でも住みたいテナントが多い。ただし利回りが低い。 改装できる物件が投資に最適	0.5%～1%	2%～3%	サンタモニカ、ハモサビーチ、マリナデルレイ、など。
A⁻	優良エリア 探せばCAP4%以上の物件もある。 このエリアの物件も改装できる物件があれば、取り込める案件となる。	1%～1.5%	3%～3.5%	レドンドビーチ、アーバイン、ウエストロサンゼルス、スタジオシティー、など。
B⁺	準優良エリア 平均値以上。物件と場所によってはA⁻になり得る物件あり。	1.5%～2%	3.5%～4%	トーランス、カルバーシティーなど。
B	極めて一般的で平均的エリア 物件によってはB⁺になり得る。	2%～2.5%	4%～4.5%	トーランス・サンペドロの一部 ノースリッジ、など。
B⁻	準平均エリア 投資としてはこのランクまでとしたい。	2.5%～3%	4.5%～5%	ノースハリウッドの一部など。
C	投資には不適格	5%～8%	6%以上	パームデール、ランキャスター等。

注意：たとえばトーランス市はかなり広い街で、A⁻のところもあれば、避けたいエリアCのところもあります。同じ市でもどの場所かということでロケーションランクが違いますので、留意する必要があります。

ントは、不動産の決定的要因は何かと尋ねますと、「Location（ロケーション）」と必ず言います。それだけロケーション（場所）は、アメリカ不動産投資におきまして、大事であるということになります。

簡単な例をあげますと、優良エリアのボロ家と治安の悪いエリアのピカピカ豪邸とではどちらが価値があるのかおわかりですか？　答えは明白です。エリア、ロケーションは最も重要で決定的な条件といえるのです。アメリカ不動産投資においては、ロケーションさえ押さえれば失敗はしません。プロの投資家は、ロケーションを絶対に外しません。もちろん、将来性を見越して未開発のエリアを開発し、莫大な利益を得るデベロッパーもありますが、通常は優良ロケーション物件でしっかりした投資を実行しています。

まずは、優良なロケーションの物件を選んでください。日本の大勢の人が追い求めているところが、必ずしもロケーションの良い物件とは限りません。本当に良いロケーションであるかどうかは、地元の信頼できる情報を元にして、しっかりと見極めてください。

いかにロケーションの悪いところの物件に価値が見出せないか、お話したいと思います。2007年のサブプライム問題、2008年のリーマンショック後に不動産市況は急落し、多くの物件が抵当権流れになりました。銀行は大量の不良債権（ローンが支払えず

第1章
ロケーションがすべて

物件が差し押さえられる)を抱え、銀行はローンを回収しようと物件をオークションで売却しました。筆者もオークションに参加しましたが、その時の物件数は数百から数千件にも上り、物件のリストが本のようにぶ厚かったことを覚えています。

オークション前にそのリストを手に入れ、目ぼしい物件を探しましたが、たった2～3件しかなく、ほとんどがとんでもないロケーションの物件でした。ちなみに、ロサンゼルスのダウンタウンから北へ車で2時間近くのところのコンベンションセンターで、オークションに行きましたが、場所はロサンゼルス・ダウンタウンのコンベンションセンターで、体育館のような広い会場でした。大勢の人だかりで、おそらく1000人以上はいたと思います。その広い会場の正面画面に、次々にオークション物件が出てきました。最初からロケーションの悪いところの物件ばかりで、スタートのビッド金額も1万ドル、2万ドル程度でしたが、誰も手を上げません。多少良さそうなロケーションの物件が出てきて、やっとオークションらしくなりましたが、全然盛り上がりません。

筆者が目をつけていた物件は、トーランス市とグレンデール市の2物件でした。最初にグレンデール市の一軒家で、午後になってやっとこれらの物件が出てきました。物件が画面に出ますと、たくさんの人がいっせいにビッドし、あっという間に50万ドル、60万ドルぐらいに上がりました。大変な盛り

35

上がりで、最終的には80万ドルぐらいで落ちたようですが、これでは普通のマーケットで購入する価格と大差がないどころか、むしろ高いくらいです。もう1件、トーランスの1LDK物件は午後遅く出ましたが、たくさんの人がビッドし、筆者も競争しましたが、結局こちらも市場価格以上に、確か20万ドル以上に上がりましたので、見過ごしました。

このようにPalmdaleやLancasterの物件は誰も見向きもしなかった一方で、グレンデールやトーランスの物件は、市場レベルの価格以上に跳ね上がったのです。Palmdaleや Lancasterの物件は、暴落する前は20万ドルから30万ドルで売られていました。90％以上も落ちても誰も買おうとはしませんでした。これが現実の実態なのです。ロケーションの悪い物件は落ちるところまで落ちてしまいますが、良いところの物件は市場レベル以上の価格が付いて売却されるのです。いかにロケーションが大事であるかがわかります。

アメリカでは、ロケーションの区別で大きく分けて、Aロケーション、Bロケーション、Cロケーションと3つのエリアに分類されます。Aは優良エリア、Bは平均的まずまず大丈夫なエリア、Cは避けたいエリアです。したがいまして、Cロケーションの物件は、問題外ということになります。では、AとBのロケーションでは、どのようにランク分けされどのような内容になるのか？　AおよびBロケーションは、それぞれ「A⁺（プラス）」、「A」、「A⁻（マイナス）」、「B⁺（プラス）」、「B」、「B⁻（マイナス）」と細分されます。ちょ

第1章
ロケーションがすべて

うど会社の格付けと同じです。では、それぞれの内容と基準点について述べます。

①「A⁺」ロケーション

空室率は、0〜0.5％。新しいテナントは、通常0日から5日ぐらいでみつかるエリアです。"0日"というのは、前テナントが退去した翌日に入居するということ（リース契約日が翌日付けで実際の入居は3〜5日後）ですが、これは物件を確保したいということで、契約を翌日付けで物件をおさえるということになります。それだけ、どうしても欲しい物件ということで、次の入居希望者が待っている物件です。誰もが住みたい最高のエリアということです。代表的なところは、ビバリーヒルズ、マリブ、マンハッタンビーチなどの超一流エリア。この「A⁺」ロケーションでは、集合住宅は極めて少なく、あっても、2戸から4戸建ての住宅物件とみなされる物件です。

②「A」ロケーション

空室率0.5％から1％未満の人気のエリア。新しいテナントは、早いときは3日ぐらいで通常は5日から10日でみつかります。サンタモニカ、マリナデルレイ、ハモサビーチ、ニューポートビーチなど。

③「A⁻」ロケーション

空室率1.0〜1.5％。新しいテナントは、早ければ1週間程度で、通常は10日から2週間ほどでみつかるエリアです。ウエスト・ロサンゼルス、スタジオ・シティ、ウエストハリウッド、レドンドビーチ、ハンティントンビーチ、アーバインなど。

④「B⁺」ロケーション

空室率は、1.5％から2％。新規テナントは2週間から3週間でみつけられます。トーランス、カルバーシティなど。

⑤「B」ロケーション

空室率2％〜2.5％。新規テナントは、半月から1か月ぐらいでみつかるエリア。トーランスの一部、サンペドロ、ノースリッジ、アナハイムなど。

もうすでにお気づきかと思いますが、各ロケーションのランクと空室率が密接にリンクしています。ロケーションが良ければ良いほど、空室率は低くなります。極めて当然の話です。筆者のお客様が購入されたロケーションが「A⁺」物件、3戸物件の小型アパートの

第1章
ロケーションがすべて

1室を新しいテナント募集の際、相場の賃料が30％以上も上がっていてびっくりした記憶があります。物件のロケーションは、ビーチに徒歩数秒で行ける絶好のエリアにあります。

また、ロケーションが良ければ利回りも低くなります。実は、ここがアメリカ不動産の一番のポイントで、利回りを優先的に追い求め物件を購入した人は、たいてい失敗しています。利回りを追求するあまり、アメリカ不動産で最も大事なエリア・ロケーションのことをつい忘れがちになります。地元の人が「よくそんなところの物件を買いましたね。地元の者ならとても手を出さない」と話す物件を購入して失敗します。利回りは二の次三の次です。

まずはロケーションをおさえることです。どうしても利回りを求める場合は、第6章で解説します改装（リフォーム）を施し、利回りを押し上げることはできます。また、ロケーションの良いところの物件は、自然と賃料も上がります。すると、利回りは改善しますし、資産価値も上がって売却益も増えることになります。

また、ロケーションのランクは同じ市でも、位置によって細分化されます。たとえば、サンタモニカでもビーチのそば、海が見えるところは「A$^+$」ですが、ビーチから離れて海が見えないところは「A」または「A$^-$」になります。

2 各エリアのロケーション

① サンタモニカ

有名な街ですね。確かに人気のあるエリアですが、実は物件オーナーには悪名高い「レント・コントロール」があります。レントの上昇率が抑えられていて、市当局が毎年レント上昇率を決めます。最近は1％以下です。長年住んでいるテナントはマーケット水準より50％以下の家賃というところが多く、あまりにも低い賃料のため、利回りは低くなります。新しくテナントを募集する場合は、マーケットレベルでのレントで募集できますが、すでに入居済みの場合には、毎年更新の際、レント・コントロールでのレントの値上げ率しか、値上げができません。したがって、サンタモニカ物件購入には、レントの実額をチェックする必要があります。ロケーションは、「A+」、「A」、「A-」の3段階に細分化されます。

② ビバリーヒルズ

ビバリーヒルズにも「レント・コントロール」があります。ただし、サンタモニカほど賃料の値上げ率は厳しくはないのですが（年率2～3％程度）、テナントが退去する費用を家主が負担することもありますので、注意が必要です。ロケーションは、「A^+」、「A^-」の2段階です。「A^+」のエリアは、北部の山を登っていくところとなりますが、集合住宅・アパートはまず存在しません。一軒家ばかりです。ハリウッドスターの家が立ち並んでいる区域です。

③ ウエスト・ハリウッド

ここは、日本ではゲイの街ということで有名ですが、ビバリーヒルズの隣に位置し、こちらでは余裕のあるロシア人が多く居住している街として知られております。「B^+」から「A^-」のロケーションですが、東側は「B」ロケーションです。

④ ウエスト・ロサンゼルス

パームズ、マーヴィスタ、ビバリーグレンなどに細分化され、ランクとして「B」から「A^-」です。サンタモニカおよびビバリーヒルズに近いエリアは、「A^-」ロケーションです。

⑤ ベニス

サンタモニカの南隣のビーチ地域で、以前は風紀が乱れる傾向にあって評判はよくなかったのですが、最近は街がきれいになって、人気があります。「B⁺」から「A⁻」。

⑥ カルバーシティ

サンタモニカやウエスト・ロサンゼルスが高騰したため、ロス空港に近いこのカルバーシティに人が増えていて、賃料・物件価格は上昇基調にあります。「B」から「B⁺」。

⑦ マリナ・デル・レイ

最大のヨットハーバーの街。ほとんどの人は、ヨットハーバーのところの物件を注目しますが、一番海寄りに小さな半島のようなところがあって、そこにはビーチフロントやオーシャンビューの物件が立ち並んでいます。一戸建てから2～4戸建てまでの投資物件もあります。ビーチフロントは「A⁺」、ビーチ・海の近くは「A」。オーシャンビューがないと「A⁻」。高速道路近辺は「B⁺」。

【最新追加情報1】プラヤビスタ、プラヤデルレイ

有名なシリコンバレーの名だたるIT企業がマリナ・デル・レイ周辺のプラヤビスタやプラヤデルレイに移転してきており、その地域一体が「シリコンビーチ」といわれています。その結果、地域や周辺エリアの不動産価格や賃料が急激に上昇しています。

【最新追加情報2】イングルウッド

カルバーシティの東隣、イングルウッド市にロサンゼルスのプロフットボールチームの本拠地スタジアムが建設されており、すでに周辺の不動産価格の値上がりが始まっています。

⑧トーランス

こちらは、全体的に中流家庭が多い平均的なエリアですが、海に近いところは「A⁻」、中間地域は「B⁺」、それ以外は「B」。ただし、高速道路に近い区域は「B⁻」とかなり広く細分化されます。

⑨パロスバーデス

昔からの高級住宅街で、「A」から「Aギリギリ」。比較的古い建物が多い。

⑩ **マンハッタンビーチ**
オーシャンフロントは、「A^+」の最上級です。ビーチのすぐそば、オーシャンビューは「A」。オーシャンビューがないところで「A」。東端エリアの一部で「A^-」か。

⑪ **ハモサビーチ**
こちらは、オーシャンフロントは「A^+」。ビーチに近く、オーシャンビューがあれば、「A」から「A^+」。その他は「A」から「A^-」。

⑫ **レドンドビーチ**
レドンドビーチは、南レドンドと北レドンドに分かれます。南レドンドは、オーシャンフロント、ビーチに近い、オーシャンビューがあるところで、「A」から「A^+」。北レドンドは、ビーチから離れていることから「A^-」。

⑬ **グレンデール**
ロスのダウンタウンへ、車で10分ぐらいで行ける便利な街で、山の手のほうは「A^-」から「A」。中間エリアは「B^+」。LAダウンタウンに近いところは、「B」から「B^-」。

第1章
ロケーションがすべて

⑭ パサデナ

有名なローズパレードが行われる街。最近、全米一の大学となったパサデナ工科大学があります。北東部の一部では「B⁻」から「C」になるところもありますが、西南部は「A」から「B⁺」。

⑮ バーバンク

グレンデールの西北隣。中間所得者層の平均的エリア。「B」から「B⁺」。ただし、高速道路近辺は「B⁻」。

⑯ スタジオシティ

文字どおり、テレビスタジオのある街で、放送関係者や映画関係者が多い。「B⁺」から「A⁻」。

⑰ ノースハリウッド

スタジオシティの北隣。芸術関係者が多いのですが、北に離れていくと「B」から「B⁻」。一部、「Cギリギリ」のところもあり「B⁺」ですが、

ます。

⑱ バレンシア

ロサンゼルスのダウンタウンから北へ車で1時間強と離れていますが、きちんと都市計画されたきれいな街です。ロケーション的には「B」から「B+」ですが、きれいなところですので、すぐに気に入られます。

⑲ ロングビーチ

ロングビーチは、「C」ランクから「A」ロケーションまで幅広いエリアです。東南地域のみ、「B」から「A」まで対象となります。東南端にベルモントショア、ネイプルズというロングビーチで最高のエリアがあります。「A⁻」から「A」です。そこから少し北にカリフォルニア州立大学のロングビーチ校がありますが、その大学周辺、特に南側は、「B+」ロケーションです。

⑳ ハンティントンビーチ

サーフィン大会のある街です。ビーチに近いオーシャンビューがあれば、「A」から

第1章
ロケーションがすべて

ます。「A$^+$」。ビーチから高速道路に近づくにつれて、「A」から「B」にランクが下がっていきます。

㉑ ニューポートビーチ
オレンジ郡のビーチ街として有名。高級ショッピングセンターもあります。ビーチやオーシャンビューのあるところは、「A」から「A$^+$」。その他は「A$^-$」。

㉒ アーバイン
カリフォルニア大学アーバイン校がある都市計画に基づいた街。きれいで小さな文教都市です。「B$^+$」から「A」のロケーションです。

㉓ コスタメサ
南カリフォルニア最大のショッピングモール「サウスコーストプラザ」がある街です。中間所得者層が住む平均的なところで、「B」ロケーション。一部に、「B$^-$」のエリアもあります。

	エリア名	ランク	コメント
1	バレンシア	B〜B＋	ＬＡダウンタウンから北へ車で１時間強と離れているが、きちんと都市計画されたきれいな街
2	ノースハリウッド	B−〜B＋	スタジオ・シティーに北隣町。芸術家関係者が多い。スタジオ・シティーに近いところがB＋
3	スタジオ・シティー	B＋〜A−	文字どおり、テレビ・スタジオのある街。放送関係者や映画関係者が多い。
4	バーバンク	B−〜B＋	グレンデールの西北隣街。中間所得者層の平均的エリア
5	グレンデール	B−〜A	ＬＡダウンタウンへ車で10分ほどで行ける高級住宅街。公立校のレベルも大変良く、白人比率も高い地区。バレー地区で最も大型のショッピングモールがある。
6	パサディナ	B−〜A	RoseBowl前に行われるローズパレードが行われる街。美術館やおしゃれなブティックやカフェがあり、アーティストに人気の街。全米１位の大学となったカリフォルニア工科大学がある。地下鉄がHolly通り沿いに走っており、駅近物件が人気
7	ウエスト・ハリウッド	B＋〜A−	ゲイの街として有名だが、おしゃれなレストランやカフェが多数ある。アーティスト、ゲイ、ユダヤ系ロシア人が多い。
8	ビバリーヒルズ	A	世界的に有名な恒久住宅地。ロデオドライブなど高級なショッピング地域としても有名。北側に向かって丘の上に超高級住宅が広がる。レント・コントロールがある。
9	ウエスト・ロサンゼルス	B〜A−	パームズ、マーヴィスタ、ビバリーグレンから成り、リトル大阪と異名を取るSawteelle通り沿いには日本食レストラン、日本の学習塾が多く、安心できる街
10	カリバーシティー	B〜B＋	サンタモニカやウエスト・ロサンゼルスが高騰したため、LA空港に近いこの地域にも入居者が増えている。
11	サンタモニカ	A	ビーチで有名な街で人気のエリア。北側の地域は海沿いに高級コンドミニアム・戸建がある全米でも有数の高級住宅地。レント・コントロールがある。
12	ベニス	B＋〜A	サンタモニカの南隣のビーチ地域で人気がある。
13	マリナデルレイ	A−〜A	ヨットハーバーのある街として有名。絶好のロケーションに加え、レストラン、スーパーも多く、生活の利便性が良い。
14	マンハッタンビーチ	A	南カリフォルニアきっての高級住宅地。ビーチ沿いの傾斜地に豪華な家々が立ち並ぶ。白人の割合が90％といわれ、全米でもトップクラスの学区域と評されている。
15	ハモサビーチ	A−〜A	ビーチシティ。華やかさと静けさの同居する街。ジョギングルート、ドッグウォークなどLAの海沿い生活をご希望の方にはピッタリの街
16	レドンドビーチ	A−〜A	トーランスの西、海沿いに細長く広がる高級リゾート地区。賃貸物件は、戸建よりコンドミニアムが多いのが特徴。オーシャンビュー物件はA。ビーチから離れるとA−
17	トーランス	B−〜A−	日系企業が集中的に営業所を開設していることで知られる。日本人に人気のエリア。日本食材を扱うスーパー、レストランが多い。全体的に中流家庭が多い。エリアは細分化されている。
18	パロス・バーデス	A	眼下に海を臨む小高い丘の上に美しい住宅が広がっている者の高級住宅街
19	ランチョ・パロス・バーデス	A−〜A	パロス・バーデスの丘の頂上から西側にかけて広がる高級住宅街。日本人駐在員も多い地域。公立校のレベルは全米でもトップクラス
20	ロングビーチ	C〜A	CランクからAランク・ロケーションまである幅の広いエリア。東南端にベルモント・ショーア、ネイブルズというロングビーチで最高のエリアがある。カリフォルニア州立大学のロングビーチ校の周辺、特に南側はB＋ロケーション
21	ハンチントンビーチ	B〜A	サーフシティとして世界的にも有名なサーフィンのメッカ。海に面して高級ホテルやリゾートコンドミニアムが立ち並ぶ。
22	コスタメサ	B−〜B	南カリフォルニア最大のショッピングモール「サウスコースト・プラザ」がある街。比較的手ごろなレントのアパート。
23	アーバイン	B＋〜A	カリフォルニア大学アーバイン校がある。都市計画に基づいた街。日本、韓国、中国系などの高所得層のアジア系住民が多く住み、駐在員向けの物件が多い。
24	ニューポートビーツ	A−〜A	裕福な住民が多い最高級住宅街。おしゃれなビーチリゾートでヨーロッパを彷彿させる。気候はアーバインに比べて涼しく、高級ショッピングセンターもある。

第1章
ロケーションがすべて

図表 1-2 ロサンゼルス・エリア情報

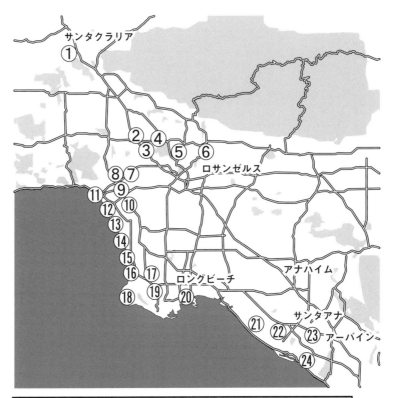

ランク	内容
A	人気の優良エリア。高い家賃でも住みたいテナントが多い
A −	優良エリア
B +	準優良エリア。平均以上
B	極めて一般的で平均的なエリア
B −	準平均的エリア。投資としてはこのランクまで
C	投資には不適格

こぼれ話 1

ニューマネー

とある情報でアメリカのFRB（連邦準備制度理事会）は、新しいマネー（仮称「eダラー」、「eマネー」など）を検討しているというか、技術的にはすでに可能のようですが、あとは世に出す方法なりタイミングやインパクトを考慮しているそうです。おそらく徐々に進めていってもう大丈夫となったころ合いを見計らって新しいお金、ニューマネーに替えると思います。

このeダラーは、現金をなくす、現金使用はしない方向でキャッシュレス時代を迎えたいということが表向きの一番の理由・背景で、現金（硬貨・紙幣）の発行コストやキャッシュ量の正確な把握が困難・煩雑になっているので、それらを一掃することが狙いだそうです。要するにシステムで管理・把握したいということです。現金を使用しないことで、不法な取引などを防ぐという効果もあります。

現在もアメリカでは、かなりのお店で銀行口座のカードやクレジットカードを使って支払いができるようになっています。少し前までは、2ドル、3ドルといった少額のやりとりはまだ現金だったのですが、今ではカードで決済ができるようになっており、明らかにキャッシュレス時代になっています。また、銀行の確認書などもペーパー

第1章
ロケーションがすべて

レスで、銀行のカードとクレジットカードですべて処理できるのは、もう間近のようです。ヨーロッパの北欧、たとえばスウェーデンでは、すべてカードや身体に埋め込まれたチップで決済しています。チップが埋め込まれた手をかざすだけで支払いは終了。キャッシュが全く不要というか、使えないそうで、旅行者がときどき困るそうです。完全なキャッシュレス社会です。

銀行もロボットやＡＩ（人工知能）を導入して人員を大幅に削減し、業務のスピード化を図ろうとしていますが、アメリカの銀行はＡＴＭマシーンやオンラインがさらに進んでいて、ほぼ機械とオンラインで処理・対応しています。いずれ銀行の支店が大幅に減少するでしょう。

世界のそういう動きのなかで、日本はいまだに現金主義で、早く対応していかないと置いてきぼりをくらいます。おそらくそうなるだろうと思います。日本の金融業界ほど、先端技術利用・採用に遅れている旧態依然としている業界はありません。キャッシュレス時代・社会はすぐ目の前です。

そのような状況にあるにもかかわらず、日本の銀行は特に３メガ銀行で向こう数年で数千人から数万人の人員削減を計画しています。しかしながら、これらは退職者数よりも少ない新規採用を抑えるということで対応するようです。またこの人員削減は、

ロボットやAIの出現で業務を大幅に縮小することで、またマイナス金利で利ざやが稼げないことが理由のようで、根本的な問題解決ではありません。

筆者が思うところ、日本に銀行はその役割を終了していると思います。戦後復興、経済成長を成し遂げるにあたり、日本の銀行は金融面で大いにサポートし助けてきましたが、おかげで日本は先進国、経済大国の仲間入りを果たしいたしました。もう役割を終了しているのです。これからはビジネス形態を根底から変えていかないと生き残れないと思います。

たとえば、ヨーロッパ、アメリカ、カナダの銀行などの金融機関は、脱化石燃料・脱炭素革命に数十兆円もの資金をすでに投下しています。バンクオブアメリカ、ING、HSBC、シティ（16兆円投資済み）JPモーガンチェイス（2025年までに22兆円投資）、トロントドミニオン、コメルツバンク、モーガンスタンリーなど。日本企業では唯一積水ハウスのみ、2016年にインドで太陽光発電のファンドに出資しています。銀行はしていません。

筆者の見るところ、近い将来銀行はなくなるのではないかと思います。もちろんいきなりなくなるのではなく、まずは支店の銀行員数が減り、次は支店が統廃合され、支店自体がどんどんなくなっていき、いずれ銀行そのものがなくなるというか、必要

第1章
ロケーションがすべて

にならなくなるのではないかと思います。少なくとも銀行は残ったとしても、支店数・銀行員数は激減すると思います。銀行業務は簡単に言えば、お金を預かり融資を行ってその金利差で商売をする、利益を稼ぐという旧態依然としたビジネス業態ですが、お金の預け入れはFRBや中央銀行でできますし、そもそもキャッシュレスになるので、預け入れは不要になるし、融資は今後クラウドファンディングやネットファンドで十分対応できるようになると思います。もちろん大企業向けの大型のファイナンスが必要になれば、日本政策銀行など政府系銀行で十分対応可能です。

そうしますと、今までの銀行は必要ではなくなります。最終的には中央銀行がすべて金融をまとめていくことになるでしょう。金融を中央銀行が握ることになれば、税金の徴収も簡単にかつ脱税などがなくなります。FRBはアメリカ全土で12地区の連銀があり、日銀も各主要都市に支店があります。

ひとつ、送金について簡単に説明致します。たとえばアメリカの知人に海外送金する場合、実際にお金を送るわけではないことは、おわかりだと思います。では具体的にどうしているかといいますと、銀行はほとんどの海外の銀行に銀行自身が口座を持っています。三菱UFJ銀行は、アメリカのJPモルガン・チェース銀行に口座があるとします。日本の三菱UFJ銀行が送金のお金を受け取り、それを自身の口座に

入金、代わり金をアメリカのチェース銀行にある三菱UFJ銀行の口座から出金し、アメリカの知人の銀行口座に送金することになります。

FRBは、新しい通貨「eダラー」を創り出し、現金を一掃すると同時に今までの通貨を新しいドルに変換する可能性は大いに考えられます。一般の経済活動や生活では、「FRBカード」なるものを発行し、すべての人(個人・法人)の口座をFRBに開設させ、それに基づいてカードを発行し、実際に支払いをする時は、指紋認証か顔認証ですべて決済させる可能性は十分ありえるでしょう。支払いの際、手をかざしたり指紋認証機に指を置くだけで、支払いは完了です。利用者はあらゆる支払いがこぶる簡単になり、いっさい現金を持ち歩くこと、使用することはなくなるでしょう。このFRB口座による一元管理は、法人・個人の経済活動というか、お金の出し入れがひと目でわかり、税金逃れも防げる効果もあります。

余談ながら、このニューマネーの「eダラー」、「eマネー」で、FRBは世界金融の元締めになりたい、世界の金融を一手に握ることを狙っていると思います。これに対するのはユーロのECB、ポンドのイングランド銀行、スイスフランのスイスなどのヨーロッパ勢です。FRBに世界の金融を牛耳られますと、FRBの思いどおりに金融を操られ、世界がFRBの言いなりになってしまう危惧があるからですが、これ

第1章
ロケーションがすべて

はユダヤ金融とキリスト教を中心とする反ユダヤ・グループの争いとも捉えられます。
この中に割って入ろうとしているのが中国ですが、世界の中国・元（げん）の地位、信用度と今後の中国経済、とくに日本同様スーパー老人大国になる中国の先行き不安があって、かなり難しい状況です。金融の元締めになれ、金融面でコントロールできます。ご存知のように、FRBはアメリカの公的機関ではなく、私企業です。オーナーは、JPモルガン・チェイス銀行、ゴールドマンサックス、ロスチャイルド銀行などで、アメリカ政府がお金がいる場合は、FRB頼みにならざるを得ないのです（詳細は自著「ドル資産を持て！」（週刊住宅新聞社刊）をご参照）。
日本の円は、こういう世界の流れや動きの対応が遅れたり誤ったりしますと、取り残されてしまう恐れは十分にあります。何もしなければ、円は日本にだけしか通用しないことにもなりかねません。海外に行く場合、たちどころに困るでしょう。今羽田や成田空港で円をドルやユーロに交換していますが、ドルもユーロもキャッシュ現金がなくなりますので、交換できなくなります。そのまま日本円を海外に持って行っても使用できなかったり通用しないでしょう。
2017年終盤に日本の代表的広告会社がアンケートをとった結果、51・6％がキャッシュレス社会に否定的とのことでした。

これから近い将来キャッシュレスや銀行がない社会になれば、どうすれば良いのでしょうか？　何が重要になるのでしょうか？　答えは「現物資産」です。

キャッシュレスになって麻薬問題がなくなると期待されますが、そう簡単に取引自体がなくなるとは思えません。おそらくキャッシュの代わりに金（ゴールド）やダイヤモンドなどの貴金属が使われると予想されます。

このように考え予想していきますと、当然ながら不動産、金（ゴールド）などの貴金属が重要な資産になります。つまり現物ですね。筆者もゴールドを買い増ししています。

購入の注意点は、ゴールドはいざというときのためのものですので、あまり高額なゴールドは使用に適しません。たとえば、飲み物や食べ物、日用品の購入には1000円、5000円、1万円で足りますので、それぐらいのゴールド、つまりコインをお勧めします。1000円相当のゴールドを50枚（5万円）から100枚（10万円分）、5000円相当のコインを10枚（5万円）ぐらい、1万円相当のコインを10枚から20枚程度は準備しておきたいものです。あとは資産の一部として50万円から100万円相当のゴールドバー（延べ棒）を3本から5本程度所有しておけば安心できます。

56

第2章 アメリカ不動産の空室リスク

1 空室リスクはない

ロケーションの良い物件を選びますと、むしろ、すぐにテナントはみつかっているといっても過言ではありません。理由はロケーションが良ければ良いほど、「入居したい」「住みたい」と希望するテナントが多いのです。もちろん家賃の額にもよりますが、できればより良いところに住みたい想いは誰しもが同じです。

筆者のお客様で、ビーチから徒歩数十秒に3戸建てアパートを所有されている方がいますが、新しいテナントを最短で0日（募集したその日に決定）、最長でも10日でみつけております。ビーチと3戸建てアパートまでの間には、5軒しか家がありません。また、窓やパティオ（中庭）からはオーシャンビューで、最高のロケーションです。

新しいテナント募集期間は最長で2か月ですが、これは申込者をかなり厳正に選択したからです。筆者の物件も、最長で3か月半かかりました、というよりもかけました。テナント選定は難しいところがあります。いったん選んでしまいますと、そう簡単に出て行っ

てくれませんので、慎重に選ぶべきでしょう。しかしながら適正な賃料でロケーションの良い物件であれば、すぐにテナントはみつかります。なお、平均募集期間は1か月程度です。

図表2-1、図表2-2をご覧ください。ロサンゼルスのアパートの平均空室率です。一番高かった年10％弱、ここ最近は3％ほどですが、これはあくまでも平均空室率です。「平均」というのは、すべてのロケーションの物件空室率ですから、ロケーションの良い物件に限ればもっと低くなります。前章のロケーション水準表に空室率も併記していますが、ロケーションの良いところの空室率は1％前後です。しかもこの率は新しいテナントがみつかるまでの期間がベースになっていますので、実質的にはゼロに限りなく近いのです。つまり空室期間は、ほとんどないのです。

図表2-3は、ロサンゼルスの中心地区の空室率です。一番低いのはPico-La Cienega地区で、2％から4％の間です。

ロサンゼルスのここ最近の平均空室率は3％ほどです。日本のように、空室が何か月も続くということはありません。仮に何か月も空いている物件があっても、それは売却用で、賃貸物件ではありません。ロサンゼルスの住宅は賃貸が約60％といわれており、賃貸需要は高く、常にあります。したがって、空室リスクもないといえます。

図表 2-1 ロサンゼルスの空室率

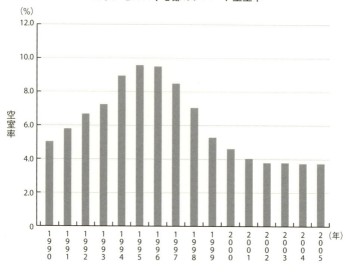

	2016	2015	2014
分譲住宅空室率	1.1%	1.2%	1.2%
賃貸住宅空室率	3.6%	4.1%	4.5%

出所：Tierra Properties。FT Journal。

第2章
アメリカ不動産の空室リスク

図表 2-2 ロサンゼルスの空室率

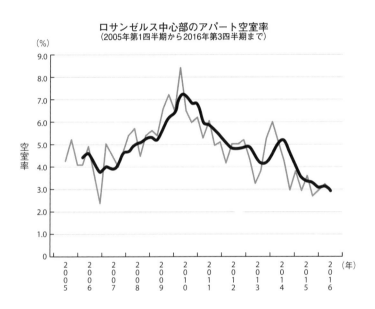

出所：アメリカ国勢調査

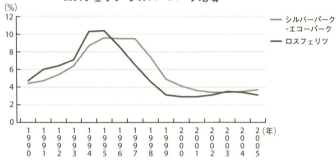

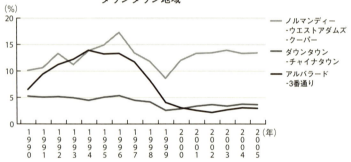

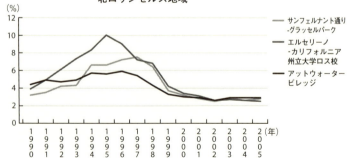

第2章
アメリカ不動産の空室リスク

図表 2-3 ロサンゼルス中心部のアパート空室率

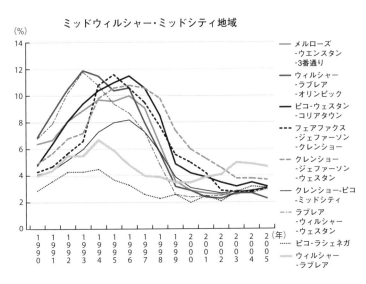

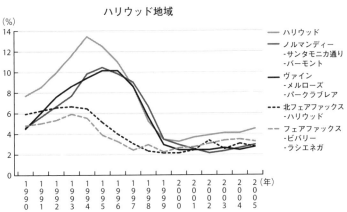

図表 2-4 カリフォルニア州の賃貸空室率推移

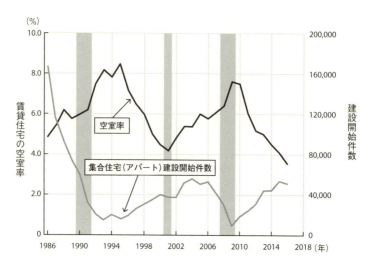

出所：アメリカ国勢調査

2 テナント属性

ロケーションの良いところの物件を取得すれば、当然家賃も高くなります。よくできているもので、賃貸者は所得に見合ったそれぞれのエリアに住み分かれます。低所得者層は家賃の低いところ、高額所得者層は家賃の高いところ、中間所得者層はその中間帯のエリアに居住します。所得が高くなればなるほど、ロケーションの良いところを選びます。

また、所得が高くなればなるほど、学歴も高く教養があるということで、テナントとしての質が高いといえます。もちろん例外はありますが、総じてそのようにいえると思います。学歴が高いということは、賃貸に限らず契約書の内容をよく理解し、その約定どおりに行い、とんでもないことを要求してきたりすることはありません。マナーも良く、要するに常識人です。しっかりした内容の契約書を取り交わせば、大きな問題になることはありません。

具体的には、低所得者層のエリアでは、常識では考えられないようなことが起こります。

テナントが赤ちゃんの使用済みオムツをトイレに流そうとしないで、収集所に直接放り投げたり、ゴミをゴミ袋に入れないできなくなったりします。

これに対し高額所得者層は、きちんと家賃を支払って、何かがこわれたりしたら家主に修理を依頼します。修理が完了するまで家賃を滞納するというような非常識で契約約定外のことは、ほとんどありません。

「そんなに高い家賃が払えるなら、家を買ったほうが良いのでは？」とよく言う人がいますが、実はアメリカではローンがおりないケースが多いのです。また、ロケーションの良い物件は高額物件ですので、購入するには最低でも10％近く必要とされる頭金も、それ相当の額になります。

アメリカでは、住宅ローンを申請してローンがおりる、承認されるのは、10人に2人〜3人だけです。あとの7人〜8人はローンがおりないのです。なぜそんなにローン承認されるのが少ないのか？　といいますと、承認条件がいくつもあって、そのなかには簡単には満たせない条件もあるからです。住宅ローンを提供するアメリカの銀行は、政府系の住宅金融公社であるフレディーマック（Freddie Mac）およびファニーメイ（Fannie Mae）の保証ないしはローン債権買取になるため、その2公社の融資条件でローン審査をして融

第2章
アメリカ不動産の空室リスク

資する、しないを決定します。その条件のなかに、「2年以上の勤務年数」があるのですが、アメリカでは収入が多い人ほど、より高収入の職場を求めて転職しますので、勤務年数が短い特徴があります。クレジット履歴が良く、収入も高いなど、条件を次々にクリアーするのですが、この2年以上の勤務年数に引っかかる人が意外と多いのです。

こういったローンが取れなかった人たちはどうするかといいますと、たいていその条件をクリアーするまで待つか、少し条件の落ちる（たとえば金利が高くなるなど）ローンを取るかに分かれます。

条件をクリアーするまで待つ人たちは、それまで家賃の高い優良ロケーションの賃貸物件を借ります。子どもを優良学校にできるだけ早く通わせたいなどが主な理由で、ローン条件をクリアーすれば、ローンを組んで物件購入に動きます。頭金をそろえるのも同様です。

このように物件のロケーションが良ければ良いほど、高額所得者層がテナントになるので、問題が起こりにくくなるというより、ほとんどありません。

こぼれ話 2

グローバル・バンクHSBC

HSBC香港上海銀行は、世界最古の銀行のひとつで、現在は世界のローカル・バンクをめざして、世界各地で支店を張り巡らしています。こぼれ話1の「ニューマネー」で申し上げました「将来銀行はなくなる」という状況のなかで、HSBCが狙っているのは、世界に支店網を築いていくことは、真逆の方向のようにみられますが、HSBCが狙っているのは、金融システムや銀行網が未発達・発展途上の国や地域に、銀行や金融サービスを張り巡らし、世界の金融をコントロールするという野望をもっているものとみられます。

また欧米の銀行などの金融機関は、これからさらに厳しく求められる環境問題解決のために、脱炭素革命・脱化石燃料のプロジェクトなどにどんどん投資しています。例をあげれば、中東などの太陽光エネルギーの太陽光パネルを砂漠に敷き詰めるなどをしています。本来の銀行業務とかけ離れた事業などに投資しているのです。HSBCはもちろんのこと、ING、UBS、JPモルガン、シティバンクなどなど。日本の銀行は投資していないことは、「こぼれ話1」で述べたとおりです。

銀行と送金について少しお話致します。

第2章
アメリカ不動産の空室リスク

ドバイの建設ラッシュは続いていますが、現地での建設労働者のほとんどは、インドからの出稼ぎ人で、ドバイで得た収入をインドの実家に送金するのですが、実は彼らは銀行口座を持っていないので、銀行ではなく両替所などにもある送金機関のオフィスに行って送金します。先進国の人たちはほとんど銀行口座を持っていますが、発展途上国の人たちで銀行口座を持っている人は少ないのです。

ドバイの送金所にドバイの通貨の給料、現金を持って行きます。そこでドバイの通貨からインドのルピーに両替してインドへ送金しますが、銀行口座がないので、銀行に送金するわけではありません。ではどうやって送金するのでしょうか？ それはその同じ送金機関のインドのオフィスに送金します。送金し終わったインド人は、故郷のインド人に送金したことを知らせます。連絡をうけたインド人は、インドにあるその送金機関のオフィスに受取人に教えます。本人確認と送金された情報、送金人、金額などがに受取人に教えます。本人確認と送金された情報、送金人、金額などが確認されますと、その場でインド・ルピーの現金を受け取ることができます。早い場合は同日、遅くとも翌日受け取れます。日本の銀行の海外送金より早く受け取れます。

それで、この送金サービスを提供している機関は、ウエスタン・ユニオン、マネーグラムといった送金サービス機関で、世界に窓口やオフィスがたくさんあります。ア

メリカでは銀行内にあるケースもあります。送金手数料は、1000ドル相当未満を送る場合20ドル程度だったと記憶しています。日本の銀行の海外送金手数料よりも安価ですね。また、よく利用する場合は、カスタマー番号などをもらって、その番号でさらに手数料は下がるようで、ドバイのインド人は皆さん利用していたようです。

この送金サービスは、何もドバイに限ったことではなく、世界中どこでも利用されています。ここで言いたいことは、銀行口座がなくても送金できる（かつ安価に）ということと、銀行の役目のうちの送金サービスは他の機関のサービスでこと足り、かつ安価で早いということで、銀行の送金業務は不要になるということです。とくに日本の銀行は？　ということです。

第3章 アメリカ不動産と訴訟

1 訴訟

「アメリカは訴訟社会だから、テナントなどから訴えられるのは避けたいので、アメリカ不動産投資はしない」という声をよく耳にします。確かにアメリカは訴訟社会ですが、売買や賃貸の不動産取引のみならず、通常の商取引においても、きちんと契約で約定されます。そう簡単に訴訟できる余地はないのです。とはいうものの、訴訟される場合も完全に否定できないので、そのためにも、あらゆるステップを踏まえて訴訟される可能性を最小限に留めます。

賃貸においてテナントからの訴訟を防ぐというか、なくす手立ては、きちんと対応できます。次の3段階で、訴訟はほぼ未然に防ぐことができます。

① テナント申込者のスクリーニング
② 賃貸借契約書

③ 保険

訴訟は未然に防ぐことはできるのですが、その前に第1章で述べたようにロケーションの良い物件を取得すれば、属性の高いテナントが見込めますので、この段階ですでに訴訟のリスクは激減されています。属性の良いテナントは、賃貸借契約を結ぶ際に、その契約内容を理解していることになります。契約内容を逸脱することはない、ということです。この点はアメリカ社会の特長で、日本のように道義的責任とか社会的責任というような概念はなく、すべて契約で明確にするという社会です。ただ融通を利かせることもあって、できる限りテナントとの関係を友好にしています。

① テナント希望者のスクリーニング

入居希望者の申込書のみならず、クレジット履歴チェックも行い、信用力がある、賃料の支払能力がしっかりしていることを、まず最初に調べますが、同時に経歴などをチェックし、変わったところがないかどうかもチェックします。新しいテナント募集のリーシングは、不動産エージェントや物件管理会社が行いますが、彼らのコメントや推薦をもらってオーナーが最終決断をします。経験豊富なエージェントや管理会社のリーシング担当者

は、申込書と履歴を見ただけでたいてい判断できるようで、必要であれば面接もします。彼らのプロとしての意見を重視・尊重し、十分話し合ってからテナントを選定することをお勧めします。このスクリーニング段階で、訴訟されるリスクはさらに低くなっています。

②賃貸借契約書

選び抜いた申込者と賃貸借契約書を取り交わしますが、この賃貸借契約書がすべての事柄について約定しますので、極めて重要です。

図表3－1の賃貸借契約書とそのコメントをご覧ください。一番重要な項目は36番の保険の項目です。

まず盗難などが原因で、テナントの所有物やテナントおよびゲストの自動車が喪失しても、家主や管理会社、エージェント、HOAの保険ではカバーしていないことを了解させていますし、テナント自身がレンターズ保険に加入しておくことを強く勧めています。

また、テナントが家主側のケガなどの補償をカバーする保険に加入することもあります。この唯一の問題は、物件の状態が良くなかったために、テナントおよびゲストがケガをした場合です。たとえば家主側の責任で、階段の手すりが緩んでいたために転んでケガをしたなどです。これは、次に述べます家主の保険でカバーすることになります。

③ 保険

最後まで問題解決に至らなかった場合は、保険で最終的にカバーすることになりますが、保険会社が調査したりなど、すべて解決してくれます。問題が発生したら、ただちに保険会社またはエージェントに通知・報告すれば、あとは保険会社が処理してくれます。

もし、保険でカバーできない、またはカバー以上のことをテナントから求められれば、示談にするか、裁判で争うかになります。裁判で争うことになって始めて弁護士に相談することになります。それまでは保険会社が対応してくれます。

最終的には補償金額で争いますので、最初に十分な補償金額の保険を手当てすればよいのですが、当然ながら支払い保険額が増えますので、その点は物件管理者やエージェントと相談すべきです。

以上のように対処すれば、弁護士を立てて裁判で争うこと、訴訟などほぼ皆無といえるのです。

やはりロケーションの良い物件であればこそ、訴訟にまで発展する可能性は極めて低くなります。

この日付は本賃貸契約書が作成された日付け

物件：物件住所など。

期間： いつから（開始日）
　　　 Aは月極め
　　　 Bはリース

家賃：家賃の金額と支払日。支払い方法など。

預かり金(敷金)：預かり金額。この預かり金は、テナントが退去後21日以内に返金しなければならない。
ただし、テナントが損害をかけた分は差引かれる。

第3章
アメリカ不動産と訴訟

図表 3-1 賃貸借契約書

CALIFORNIA ASSOCIATION OF REALTORS®

RESIDENTIAL LEASE OR MONTH-TO-MONTH RENTAL AGREEMENT
(C.A.R. Form LR, Revised 6/17)

Date _05/15/2018_

Taro Nippon ("Landlord") and _John Tenant_ ("Tenant") agree as follows:

1. **PROPERTY:**
   A. Landlord rents to Tenant and Tenant rents from Landlord, the real property and improvements described as: _1234 Sample Street, Sample, CA 90000_ ("Premises").
   B. The Premises are for the sole use as a personal residence by the following named person(s) only _Jon Tenant and Mary Tenant_.
   C. The following personal property, maintained pursuant to paragraph 11, is included: _____ or ☐ (if checked) the personal property on the attached addendum.
   D. The Premises may be subject to a local rent control ordinance

2. **TERM:** The term begins on (date) _June 1, 2018_ ("Commencement Date"). If Tenant has not paid all amounts then due; (i) Tenant has no right to possession or keys to the premises and (ii) this Agreement is voidable at the option of Landlord, 2 calendar days after giving Tenant a Notice to Pay (C.A.R. Form PPN). Notice may be delivered to Tenant (i) in person; (ii) by mail to Tenant's last known address; or (iii) by email, if provided in Tenant's application or previously used by Tenant to communicate with Landlord or agent for Owner. If Landlord elects to void the lease, Landlord shall refund to Tenant all rent and security deposit paid.
   (Check A or B):
   ☐ A. **Month-to-Month:** This Agreement continues from the commencement date as a month-to-month tenancy. Tenant may terminate the tenancy by giving written notice at least 30 days prior to the intended termination date. Tenant shall be responsible for paying rent through the termination date even if moving out early. Landlord may terminate the tenancy by giving written notice as provided by law. Such notices may be given on any date.
   ☒ B. **Lease:** This Agreement shall terminate on (date) _May 31, 2019_ at _11:59_ ☐AM/☒PM. Tenant shall vacate the Premises upon termination of the Agreement, unless: **(i)** Landlord and Tenant have extended this Agreement in writing or signed a new agreement; **(ii)** mandated by local rent control law; or **(iii)** Landlord accepts Rent from Tenant (other than past due Rent), in which case a month-to-month tenancy shall be created which either party may terminate as specified in paragraph 2A. Rent shall be at a rate agreed to by Landlord and Tenant, or as allowed by law. All other terms and conditions of this Agreement shall remain in full force and effect.

3. **RENT:** "Rent" shall mean all monetary obligations of Tenant to Landlord under the terms of the Agreement, except security deposit.
   A. Tenant agrees to pay $ _2,500.00_ per month for the term of the Agreement.
   B. Rent is payable in advance on the **1st (or** ☐ **)** day of each calendar month, and is delinquent on the next day.
   C. If Commencement Date falls on any day other than the day Rent is payable under paragraph 3B, and Tenant has paid one full month's Rent in advance of Commencement Date, Rent for the second calendar month shall be prorated and Tenant shall pay 1/30th of the monthly rent per day for each day remaining in prorated second month.
   D. PAYMENT: **(1)** Rent shall be paid by ☐ personal check, ☐ money order, ☐ cashier's check, made payable to _ABC Property Management Company_ ☒ wire/electronic transfer, or ☒ other _Direct Deposit, or Bill Pay_.
   (2) Rent shall be delivered to (name) _ABC Property Management Company_
   (whose phone number is) _____ at (address) _____
   _____, (or at any other location subsequently specified by Landlord in writing to Tenant)
   (and ☐ if checked, rent may be paid personally, between the hours of _____ and _____ on the following days _____).
   (3) If any payment is returned for non-sufficient funds ("NSF") or because Tenant stops payment, then, after that: (i) Landlord may, in writing, require Tenant to pay Rent in cash for three months and (ii) all future Rent shall be paid by ☒ money order, or ☒ cashier's check.
   E. Rent payments received by Landlord shall be applied to the earliest amount(s) due or past due.

4. **SECURITY DEPOSIT:**
   A. Tenant agrees to pay $ _3,000.00_ as a security deposit. Security deposit will be ☐ transferred to and held by the Owner of the Premises, or ☒ held in Owner's Broker's trust account.
   B. All or any portion of the security deposit may be used, as reasonably necessary, to: **(i)** cure Tenant's default in payment of Rent (which includes Late Charges, NSF fees or other sums due); **(ii)** repair damage, excluding ordinary wear and tear, caused by Tenant or by a guest or licensee of Tenant; **(iii)** clean Premises, if necessary, upon termination of the tenancy; and **(iv)** replace or return personal property or appurtenances. **SECURITY DEPOSIT SHALL NOT BE USED BY TENANT IN LIEU OF PAYMENT OF LAST MONTH'S RENT.** If all or any portion of the security deposit is used during the tenancy, Tenant agrees to reinstate the total security deposit within five days after written notice is delivered to Tenant. Within 21 days after Tenant vacates the Premises, Landlord shall: **(1)** furnish Tenant an itemized statement indicating the amount of any security deposit received and the basis for its disposition and supporting documentation as required by California Civil Code § 1950.5(g); and **(2)** return any remaining portion of the security deposit to Tenant.
   C. **Security deposit will not be returned until all Tenants have vacated the Premises and all keys returned. Any security deposit returned by check shall be made out to all Tenants named on this Agreement, or as subsequently modified.**
   D. **No interest will be paid on security deposit unless required by local law.**
   E. If the security deposit is held by Owner, Tenant agrees not to hold Broker responsible for its return. If the security deposit is held in Owner's Broker's trust account, and Broker's authority is terminated before expiration of this Agreement, **and** security deposit is released to someone other than Tenant, **then** Broker shall notify Tenant, in writing, where and to whom security deposit has been released. Once Tenant has been provided such notice, Tenant agrees not to hold Broker responsible for the security deposit.

Tenant's Initials (_____) (_____)   Landlord's Initials (_____) (_____)

© 2017, California Association of REALTORS®, Inc.

LR REVISED 6/17 (PAGE 1 OF 7)
RESIDENTIAL LEASE OR MONTH-TO-MONTH RENTAL AGREEMENT (LR PAGE 1 OF 7)

- 入居時の必要金額：最初の家賃、預かり金、その他（たとえば鍵の預かり金など）がそれぞれいくらでいつの支払いかの記載

- 家賃遅延料；不渡り小切手：家賃支払いの期限日数とその遅延料。家賃支払い小切手が不渡りになった場合の救済とその損害料

- パーキング（駐車場）：パーキングは家賃に含まれるいるかどうか。含まれていない場合は、その金額を別途設定

- 倉庫：荷物置きの倉庫は家賃に含まれているかどうか。含まれていない場合は、その金額を別途設定

- 光熱費：光熱費の家主とテナントの負担分担

- 物件状態：テナントが入居時に物件状態をチェック

第3章
アメリカ不動産と訴訟

Premises: *1234 Sample Street, Sample, CA 90000*   Date: *May 15, 2018*

5. **MOVE-IN COSTS RECEIVED/DUE:** Move-in funds shall be paid by ☐ personal check, ☒ money order, or ☒ cashier's check, ☒ wire/electronic transfer.

Category	Total Due	Payment Received	Balance Due	Date Due	Payable To
Rent from *06/01/2018* to *06/30/2018* (date)	$2,500.00		$2,500.00	05/15/2018	*ABC Property Management*
*Security Deposit	$3,000.00		$3,000.00	05/15/2018	*ABC Property Management*
Other *Key Deposit*	$100.00		$100.00	05/15/2018	*ABC Property Management*
Other					
Total	$5,600.00		$5,600.00	05/15/2018	*ABC Property Management*

*The maximum amount of security deposit, however designated, cannot exceed two months' Rent for unfurnished premises, or three months' Rent for furnished premises.

6. **LATE CHARGE; RETURNED CHECKS:**
   A. Tenant acknowledges either late payment of Rent or issuance of a returned check may cause Landlord to incur costs and expenses, the exact amounts of which are extremely difficult and impractical to determine. These costs may include, but are not limited to, processing, enforcement and accounting expenses, and late charges imposed on Landlord. If any installment of Rent due from Tenant is not received by Landlord within **5** (or ☐ _____) **calendar days** after the date due, or if a check is returned, Tenant shall pay to Landlord, respectively, an additional sum of $ _____ or _**5.000**_ % of the Rent due as a Late Charge and $25.00 as a NSF fee for the first returned check and $35.00 as a NSF fee for each additional returned check, either or both of which shall be deemed additional Rent.
   B. Landlord and Tenant agree that these charges represent a fair and reasonable estimate of the costs Landlord may incur by reason of Tenant's late or NSF payment. Any Late Charge or NSF fee due shall be paid with the current installment of Rent. Landlord's acceptance of any Late Charge or NSF fee shall not constitute a waiver as to any default of Tenant. Landlord's right to collect a Late Charge or NSF fee shall neither be deemed an extension of the date Rent is due under paragraph 3 nor prevent Landlord from exercising any other rights and remedies under this Agreement and as provided by law.

7. **PARKING: (Check A or B)**
   ☒ A. Parking is permitted as follows: _**assigned garage.**_

   The right to parking ☒ is ☐ is not included in the Rent charged pursuant to paragraph 3. If not included in the Rent, the parking rental fee shall be an additional $ _____ per month. Parking space(s) are to be used only for parking properly registered and operable motor vehicles, except for trailers, boats, campers, buses or trucks (other than pick-up trucks). Tenant shall park in assigned space(s) only. Parking space(s) are to be kept clean. Vehicles leaking oil, gas or other motor vehicle fluids shall not be parked on the Premises. Mechanical work, or storage of inoperable vehicles, or storage of any kind is not permitted in parking space(s) or elsewhere on the Premises except as specified in paragraph 8.
   OR ☐ B. Parking is not permitted on the Premises.

8. **STORAGE: (Check A or B)**
   ☒ A. Storage is permitted as follows: _**in the premises and garage.**_
   The right to separate storage space ☒ is, ☐ is not, included in the Rent charged pursuant to paragraph 3. If not included in the Rent, storage space fee shall be an additional $ _____ per month. Tenant shall store only personal property Tenant owns, and shall not store property claimed by another or in which another has any right, title or interest. Tenant shall not store any improperly packaged food or perishable goods, flammable materials, explosives, hazardous waste or other inherently dangerous material, or illegal substances.
   OR ☐ B. Except for Tenant's personal property, contained entirely within the Premises, storage is not permitted on the Premises.

9. **UTILITIES:** Tenant agrees to pay for all utilities and services, and the following charges: _**Electricity, Gas, Internet, Cable TV, etc.**_ except _**Water & Trash.**_ , which shall be paid for by Landlord. If any utilities are not separately metered, Tenant shall pay Tenant's proportional share, as reasonably determined and directed by Landlord. If utilities are separately metered, Tenant shall place utilities in Tenant's name as of the Commencement Date. Landlord is only responsible for installing and maintaining one usable telephone jack and one telephone line to the Premises. Tenant shall pay any cost for conversion from existing utilities service provider.
   ☐ A. **Water Submeters:** Water use on the Premises is measured by a submeter and Tenant will be separately billed for water usage based on the submeter. See attached Water Submeter Addendum (C.A.R. Form WSM) for additional terms.
   ☐ B. **Gas Meter:** The Premises does not have a separate gas meter.
   ☐ C. **Electric Meter:** The Premises does not have a separate electrical meter.

10. **CONDITION OF PREMISES:** Tenant has examined Premises and, if any, all furniture, furnishings, appliances, landscaping and fixtures, including smoke alarm(s) and carbon monoxide detector(s).
    (Check all that apply:)
    ☐ A. Tenant acknowledges these items are clean and in operable condition, with the following exceptions: _____
    ☒ B. Tenant's acknowledgment of the condition of these items is contained in an attached statement of condition (C.A.R. Form MIMO).
    ☒ C. (i) Landlord will Deliver to Tenant a statement of condition (C.A.R. Form MIMO) ☐ within **3 days** after execution of this Agreement; ☐ prior to the Commencement Date; ☐ within **3 days** after the Commencement Date.
    (ii) Tenant shall complete and return the MIMO to Landlord within **3 (or** ☐ _____ **) days** after Delivery. Tenant's failure to return the MIMO within that time shall conclusively be deemed Tenant's Acknowledgement of the condition as stated in the MIMO.
    ☐ D. Tenant will provide Landlord a list of items that are damaged or not in operable condition within **3 (or** ☐ _____ **) days** after Commencement Date, not as a contingency of this Agreement but rather as an acknowledgement of the condition of the Premises.
    ☐ E. Other: _____

Tenant's Initials (_____) (_____)   Landlord's Initials (_____) (_____)

LR REVISED 6/17 (PAGE 2 OF 7)
RESIDENTIAL LEASE OR MONTH-TO-MONTH RENTAL AGREEMENT (LR PAGE 2 OF 7)

物件維持と報告：テナントは物件をきちんと使用・維持。庭などの手入れは家主かテナントか、など。

近隣状態：テナントは近所の迷惑にならないようにする、など。

ペット：ペットは家主との事前合意なしでは禁止

禁煙：禁煙または喫煙の場合は喫煙による損害が発生した場合は、テナントがすべての損額を負担する。

規則／規定：テナントは家主のすべての規則・規定に従う。

コンドミニアム：物件がコンドミニアムの場合、テナントは HOA（Home Owners Association＝共有組合とほぼ同じ）の規則に従う。

変更；修理：テナントは家主の事前承諾・合意なしで、勝手に物件の変更や修理はできない。

第3章
アメリカ不動産と訴訟

Premises: **1234 Sample Street, Sample, CA 90000** Date: **May 15, 2018**

11. MAINTENANCE USE AND REPORTING:
   A. Tenant shall properly use, operate and safeguard Premises, including if applicable, any landscaping, furniture, furnishings and appliances, and all mechanical, electrical, gas and plumbing fixtures, carbon monoxide detector(s) and smoke alarms, and keep them and the Premises clean, sanitary and well ventilated. Tenant shall be responsible for checking and maintaining all carbon monoxide detectors and any additional phone lines beyond the one line and jack that Landlord shall provide and maintain. Tenant shall immediately notify Landlord, in writing, of any problem, malfunction or damage with any item including carbon monoxide detector(s) and smoke alarms on the property. Tenant shall be charged for all repairs or replacements caused by Tenant, pets, guests or licensees of Tenant, excluding ordinary wear and tear. Tenant shall be charged for all damage to Premises as a result of failure to report a problem in a timely manner. Tenant shall be charged for repair of drain blockages or stoppages, unless caused by defective plumbing parts or tree roots invading sewer lines.
   B. ☐ Landlord ☐ Tenant shall water the garden, landscaping, trees and shrubs, except: _____
   C. ☐ Landlord ☐ Tenant shall maintain the garden, landscaping, trees and shrubs, except: _____
   D. ☐ Landlord ☒ Tenant shall maintain _the premises including the garage clean and use in proper way._
   E. Landlord and Tenant agree that State or local water use restrictions shall supersede any obligation of Landlord or Tenant to water or maintain any garden, landscaping, trees or shrubs pursuant to 11B, 11C, and 11D.
   F. Tenant's failure to maintain any item for which Tenant is responsible shall give Landlord the right to hire someone to perform such maintenance and charge Tenant to cover the cost of such maintenance.
   G. The following items of personal property are included in the Premises without warranty and Landlord will not maintain, repair or replace them: _Washer & Dryer, and Refrigerator._
   H. Tenant understands that if Premises is located in a Common Interest Development, Landlord may not have authority or control over certain parts of the Premises such as roof, electrical, gas or plumbing features inside certain walls, and common areas such as shared parking structure or garage.
   I. Tenant shall not use the premises to plant, grow, cultivate or sell marijuana.

12. NEIGHBORHOOD CONDITIONS: Tenant is advised to satisfy him or herself as to neighborhood or area conditions, including, but not limited to, schools, proximity and adequacy of law enforcement, crime statistics, proximity of registered felons or offenders, fire protection, other governmental services, availability, adequacy and cost of any wired, wireless internet connections or other telecommunications or other technology services and installations, proximity to commercial, industrial or agricultural activities, existing and proposed transportation, construction and development that may affect noise, view, or traffic, airport noise, noise or odor from any source, wild and domestic animals, other nuisances, hazards, or circumstances, cemeteries, facilities and condition of common areas, conditions and influences of significance to certain cultures and/or religions, and personal needs, requirements and preferences of Tenant.

13. PETS: Unless otherwise provided in California Civil Code §54.2, no animal or pet shall be kept on or about the Premises without Landlord's prior written consent, ☐ except as agreed to in the attached Pet Addendum (C.A.R. Form PET).

14. NO SMOKING:
   A. (i) Tenant is responsible for all damage caused by smoking including, but not limited to stains, burns, odors and removal of debris; (ii) Tenant acknowledges that in order to remove odor caused by smoking, Landlord may need to replace carpet and drapes and paint the entire premises regardless of when these items were last cleaned, replaced or repainted. Such actions and other necessary steps will impact the return of any security deposit.
   B. The Premises or common areas may be subject to a local non-smoking ordinance.
   C. NO SMOKING of any substance is allowed on the Premises or common areas. If smoking does occur on the Premises or common areas, (i) Tenant is in material breach of this Agreement; (ii) Tenant, guests, and all others may be required to leave the Premises. ☐ Smoking of the following substances only is allowed: _____

15. RULES/REGULATIONS:
   A. Tenant agrees to comply with all Landlord rules and regulations that are at any time posted on the Premises or delivered to Tenant. Tenant shall not, and shall ensure that guests and licensees of Tenant shall not, disturb, annoy, endanger or interfere with other tenants of the building or neighbors, or use the Premises for any unlawful purposes, under federal, state, or local law including, but not limited to, using, manufacturing, selling, storing or transporting illicit drugs or other contraband, or violate any law or ordinance, or commit a waste or nuisance on or about the Premises.
   B. **(If applicable, check one)**
      ☐ 1. Landlord shall provide Tenant with a copy of the rules and regulations within _____ days
      or _____
      OR ☐ 2. Tenant has been provided with and, acknowledges receipt of, a copy of the rules and regulations.

16. ☐ (If checked) **CONDOMINIUM; PLANNED UNIT DEVELOPMENT:**
   A. The Premises are a unit in a condominium, planned unit development, common interest subdivision or other development governed by a homeowners' association ("HOA"). The name of the HOA is _____. Tenant agrees to comply with all HOA covenants, conditions and restrictions, bylaws, rules and regulations and decisions ("HOA Rules"). Tenant shall reimburse Landlord for any fines or charges imposed by HOA or other authorities, due to any violation by Tenant, or the guests or licensees of Tenant or Landlord shall have the right to deduct such amounts from the security deposit.
   B. If applicable, Tenant is required to pay a fee to the HOA to gain access to certain areas within the development such as but not necessarily including or limited to the front gate, pool, and recreational facilities. If not specified in paragraph 5, Tenant is solely responsible for payment and satisfying any HOA requirements prior to or upon or after the Commencement Date.
   C. **(Check one)**
      ☐ 1. Landlord shall provide Tenant with a copy of the HOA Rules within _____ days
      or _____
      OR ☐ 2. Tenant has been provided with, and acknowledges receipt of, a copy of the HOA Rules.

17. ALTERATIONS; REPAIRS: Unless otherwise specified by law or paragraph 32C, without Landlord's prior written consent, **(i)** Tenant shall not make any repairs, alterations or improvements in or about the Premises including: painting, wallpapering, adding or changing locks, installing antenna or satellite dish(es), placing signs, displays or exhibits, or using screws, fastening devices, large nails or adhesive materials; **(ii)** Landlord shall not be responsible for the costs of alterations or repairs made by Tenant; **(iii)** Tenant shall not deduct from Rent the costs of any repairs, alterations or improvements; and **(iv)** any deduction made by Tenant shall be considered unpaid Rent.

Tenant's Initials (_____) (_____) Landlord's Initials (_____) (_____)

LR REVISED 6/17 (PAGE 3 OF 7)
RESIDENTIAL LEASE OR MONTH-TO-MONTH RENTAL AGREEMENT (LR PAGE 3 OF 7)

入室：テナントは家主または代理者が必要な修理・修繕のため24時間通知を受けて入室することを認める。

写真とインターネット広告：物件売却やレンタルの広告のため、写真とインターネット掲載をテナントは合意する。

サイン：テナントは家主が物件に売却やテナント募集のサインを認める。

譲渡：テナントの物件賃貸の譲渡禁止

共同と個人義務：テナントが複数の場合、個人すべて本契約条項すべて遵守

鉛入りペイント：1978年以前の物件の場合、鉛入りペイントの書類を締結

定期的シロアリ駆除：家主が定期的なシロアリ駆除を行う契約を駆除会社と締結している場合、テナントに通知。ただし、物件が一軒家の場合は、テナントがシロアリ駆除の責任を負う。

中枢神経障害汚染：中枢神経障害汚染の物件通知を当局から受けた場合、その通知のコピーをテナントに手渡す。

ベッド害虫［しらみ・南京虫］：家主はベッド害虫の知識はない。

ミーガン法データ開示：
ミーガン法の情報・資料はそのウェブサイトで確認可能。
［ミーガン法は性的犯罪者に関するもの］

居住環境危険パンフレット：テナントは同パンフレットを受領する。

軍隊情報公開：
物件が1マイル以内に以前軍隊の訓練が行われていた（家主が知っている）場合、公開

第3章
アメリカ不動産と訴訟

鍵；ロック：鍵の受け渡し（テナントの受領）

Premises: *1234 Sample Street, Sample, CA 90000* Date: *May 15, 2018*

18. KEYS; LOCKS:
  A. Tenant acknowledges receipt of (or Tenant will receive ☐ prior to the Commencement Date, or ☐ _____):
    [X] 2 key(s) to Premises,   [X] 2 remote control device(s) for garage door/gate opener(s),
    [X] 1 key(s) to mailbox,
    ___ key(s) to common area(s),
  B. Tenant acknowledges that locks to the Premises ☐ have, ☑ have not, been re-keyed.
  C. If Tenant re-keys existing locks or opening devices, Tenant shall immediately deliver copies of all keys to Landlord. Tenant shall pay all costs and charges related to loss of any keys or opening devices. Tenant may not remove locks, even if installed by Tenant.

19. ENTRY:
  A. Tenant shall make Premises available to Landlord or Landlord's representative for the purpose of entering to make necessary or agreed repairs (including, but not limited to, installing, repairing, testing, and maintaining smoke detectors and carbon monoxide devices, and bracing, anchoring or strapping water heaters, or repairing dilapidation relating to the presence of mold); providing decorations, alterations, or improvements, or supplying necessary or agreed services; or to show Premises to prospective or actual purchasers, tenants, mortgagees, lenders, appraisers, contractors and others (collectively "Interested Persons"). Tenant agrees that Landlord, Broker and Interested Persons may take photos of the Premises.
  B. Landlord and Tenant agree that 24-hour written notice shall be reasonable and sufficient notice, except as follows: (1) 48-hour written notice is required to conduct an inspection of the Premises prior to the Tenant moving out, unless the Tenant waives the right to such notice. (2) If Landlord has in writing informed Tenant that the Premises are for sale and that Tenant will be notified orally to show the premises (C.A.R. Form NSE), then, for the next 120 days following the delivery of the NSE, notice may be given orally to show the Premises to actual or prospective purchasers. No written notice is required if Landlord and Tenant orally agree to an entry for agreed services or repairs if the date and time of entry are within one week of the oral agreement. (4) No notice is required: (i) to enter in case of an emergency, (ii) if the Tenant is present and consents at the time of entry; or (iii) if the Tenant has abandoned or surrendered the Premises.
  C. ☐ (If checked) Tenant authorizes the use of a keysafe/lockbox to allow entry into the Premises and agrees to sign a keysafe/lockbox addendum (C.A.R. Form KLA).

20. PHOTOGRAPHS AND INTERNET ADVERTISING:
  A. In order to effectively market the Premises for sale or rental it is often necessary to provide photographs, virtual tours and other media to Interested Persons. Tenant agrees that Broker may photograph or otherwise electronically capture images of the exterior and interior of the Premises ("Images") for static and/or virtual tours of the Premises by Interested Persons for use on Broker's website, the MLS, and other marketing materials and sites. Tenant acknowledges that once Images are placed on the Internet neither Broker nor Landlord has control over who can view such Images and what use viewers may make of the Images, or how long such Images may remain available on the Internet.
  B. Tenant acknowledges that prospective Interested Persons coming onto the Premises may take photographs, videos or other images of the Premises. Tenant understands that Broker does not have the ability to control or block the taking and use of Images by any such persons. Once Images are taken and/or put into electronic display on the Internet or otherwise, neither Broker nor Landlord has control over who views such Images nor what use viewers may make of the Images.

21. SIGNS: Tenant authorizes Landlord to place FOR SALE/LEASE signs on the Premises.

22. ASSIGNMENT; SUBLETTING: A. Tenant shall not sublet all or any part of Premises, or parking or storage spaces, or assign or transfer this Agreement or any interest in it, without Landlord's prior written consent. Unless such consent is obtained, any assignment, transfer or subletting of Premises or this Agreement or tenancy, by voluntary act of Tenant, operation of law or otherwise, shall, at the option of Landlord, terminate this Agreement. Any proposed assignee, transferee or sublessee shall submit to Landlord an application and credit information for Landlord's approval and, if approved, sign a separate written agreement with Landlord and Tenant. Landlord's consent to any one assignment, transfer or sublease, shall not be construed as consent to any subsequent assignment, transfer or sublease and does not release Tenant of Tenant's obligations under this Agreement. **B.** This prohibition also applies (☐ does not apply) to short term, vacation, and transient rentals such as, but not limited to, those arranged through AirBnB, VRBO, HomeAway or other short term rental services. **C.** Any violation of this prohibition is a non-curable, material breach of the Agreement.

23. JOINT AND INDIVIDUAL OBLIGATIONS: If there is more than one Tenant, each one shall be individually and completely responsible for the performance of all obligations of Tenant under this Agreement, jointly with every other Tenant, and individually, whether or not in possession.

24. ☐ **LEAD-BASED PAINT (If checked):** Premises were constructed prior to 1978. In accordance with federal law, Landlord gives and Tenant acknowledges receipt of the disclosures on the attached form (C.A.R. Form FLD) and a federally approved lead pamphlet.

25. PERIODIC PEST CONTROL: (CHECK IF EITHER APPLIES)
  ☐ A. Landlord has entered into a contract for periodic pest control treatment of the Premises and shall give Tenant a copy of the notice originally given to Landlord by the pest control company.
  ☐ B. Premises is a house. Tenant is responsible for pest control.

26. ☐ **METHAMPHETAMINE CONTAMINATION:** Prior to signing this Agreement, Landlord has given Tenant a notice that a health official has issued an order prohibiting occupancy of the property because of methamphetamine contamination. A copy of the notice and order are attached.

27. BED BUGS: Landlord has no knowledge of any infestation in the Premises by bed bugs. See attached Bed Bug Disclosure (C.A.R. Form BBD) for further information. Tenant shall report suspected bed bug infestation to Landlord or, if applicable, property manager and cooperate with any inspection for and treatment of bed bugs. Landlord will notify tenants of any units infested by bed bugs.

28. MEGAN'S LAW DATABASE DISCLOSURE: Notice: Pursuant to Section 290.46 of the Penal Code, information about specified registered sex offenders is made available to the public via an Internet Web site maintained by the Department of Justice at www.meganslaw.ca.gov. Depending on an offender's criminal history, this information will include either the address at which the offender resides or the community of residence and ZIP Code in which he or she resides. (Neither Landlord nor Brokers, if any, are required to check this website. If Tenant wants further information, Tenant should obtain information directly from this website.)

29. ☐ **RESIDENTIAL ENVIRONMENTAL HAZARDS BOOKLET:** Tenant acknowledges receipt of the residential environmental hazards booklet.

30. ☐ **MILITARY ORDNANCE DISCLOSURE:** (If applicable and known to Landlord) Premises are located within one mile of an area once used for military training, and may contain potentially explosive munitions.

Tenant's Initials (_____) (_____)   Landlord's Initials (_____) (_____)

LR REVISED 6/17 (PAGE 4 OF 7)
RESIDENTIAL LEASE OR MONTH-TO-MONTH RENTAL AGREEMENT (LR PAGE 4 OF 7)

所有；テナントが入居日後5日以内に入居できない場合、契約をキャンセルできる。

テナントの義務（物件退去）：テナントは退去の際、鍵などをすべて家主に返却、物件を掃除

契約不履行；事前解約：
事前解約の場合、テナントは家賃の消失、不動産手数料など負担

一時的退去：シロアリ駆除などのため、テナントは一時的に退去することに合意

物件損害：地震や事故などが原因で物件居住が不可能になった場合、本賃貸契約は解約可能

保険：テナントやゲストの所有物や自動車が、盗難や犯罪などあらゆる原因で損害をこうむっても家主およびそのエージェント、またHOAの保険ではカバーされていない。テナントは、レンターズ保険で自分自身の所有物を守ることを強く求められる。また、テナントは家主に対する損害保険を手当て

ウォーター・ベッド／簡易乾燥機：ウォーター・ベッド、簡易乾燥機、および簡易洗濯機は使用できない。

放棄：いかなる契約不履行の条項を放棄することは、同条項不履行が継続した場合や、その後も発生する条項を放棄することにはならない。

通知：家主とテナントへの通知住所

テナント賃貸内容証明書：賃貸内容を確認する証明書は、家主またはそのエージェントに求められれば、テナントは3日以内に提出

表示：テナントは賃貸申請書の内容を保障

第3章
アメリカ不動産と訴訟

Premises: *1234 Sample Street, Sample, CA 90000*   Date: *May 15, 2018*

31. POSSESSION:
    A. Tenant is not in possession of the Premises. If Landlord is unable to deliver possession of Premises on Commencement Date, such Date shall be extended to the date on which possession is made available to Tenant. If Landlord is unable to deliver possession within **5 (or ☐ _____) calendar days** after agreed Commencement Date, Tenant may terminate this Agreement by giving written notice to Landlord, and shall be refunded all Rent and security deposit paid. Possession is deemed terminated when Tenant has returned all keys to the Premises to Landlord.
    B. ☐ Tenant is already in possession of the Premises.

32. TENANT'S OBLIGATIONS UPON VACATING PREMISES:
    A. Upon termination of this Agreement, Tenant shall: **(i)** give Landlord all copies of all keys and any opening devices to Premises, including any common areas; **(ii)** vacate and surrender Premises to Landlord, empty of all persons; **(iii)** vacate any/all parking and/or storage space; **(iv)** clean and deliver Premises, as specified in paragraph C below, to Landlord in the same condition as referenced in paragraph 10; **(v)** remove all debris; **(vi)** give written notice to Landlord of Tenant's forwarding address; and **(vii)**

    B. All alterations/improvements made by or caused to be made by Tenant, with or without Landlord's consent, become the property of Landlord upon termination. Landlord may charge Tenant for restoration of the Premises to the condition it was in prior to any alterations/improvements.

    C. Right to Pre-Move-Out Inspection and Repairs: (i) After giving or receiving notice of termination of a tenancy (C.A.R. Form NTT), or before the expiration of this Agreement, Tenant has the right to request that an inspection of the Premises take place prior to termination of the lease or rental (C.A.R. Form NRI). If Tenant requests such an inspection, Tenant shall be given an opportunity to remedy identified deficiencies prior to termination, consistent with the terms of this Agreement. **(ii)** Any repairs or alterations made to the Premises as a result of this inspection (collectively, "Repairs") shall be made at Tenant's expense. Repairs may be performed by Tenant or through others, who have adequate insurance and licenses and are approved by Landlord. The work shall comply with applicable law, including governmental permit, inspection and approval requirements. Repairs shall be performed in a good, skillful manner with materials of quality and appearance comparable to existing materials. It is understood that exact restoration of appearance or cosmetic items following all Repairs may not be possible. **(iii)** Tenant shall: **(a)** obtain receipts for Repairs performed by others; **(b)** prepare a written statement indicating the Repairs performed by Tenant and the date of such Repairs; and **(c)** provide copies of receipts and statements to Landlord prior to termination. Paragraph 32C does not apply when the tenancy is terminated pursuant to California Code of Civil Procedure § 1161(2), (3) or (4).

33. BREACH OF CONTRACT; EARLY TERMINATION: In addition to any obligations established by paragraph 32, in the event of termination by Tenant prior to completion of the original term of the Agreement, Tenant shall also be responsible for lost Rent, rental commissions, advertising expenses and painting costs necessary to ready Premises for re-rental. Landlord may withhold any such amounts from Tenant's security deposit.

34. TEMPORARY RELOCATION: Subject to local law, Tenant agrees, upon demand of Landlord, to temporarily vacate Premises for a reasonable period, to allow for fumigation (or other methods) to control wood destroying pests or organisms, or other repairs to Premises. Tenant agrees to comply with all instructions and requirements necessary to prepare Premises to accommodate pest control, fumigation or other work, including bagging or storage of food and medicine, and removal of perishables and valuables. Tenant shall only be entitled to a credit of Rent equal to the per diem Rent for the period of time Tenant is required to vacate Premises.

35. DAMAGE TO PREMISES: If, by no fault of Tenant, Premises are totally or partially damaged or destroyed by fire, earthquake, accident or other casualty that render Premises totally or partially uninhabitable, either Landlord or Tenant may terminate this Agreement by giving the other written notice. Rent shall be abated as of the date Premises become totally or partially uninhabitable. The abated amount shall be the current monthly Rent prorated on a 30-day period. If the Agreement is not terminated, Landlord shall promptly repair the damage, and Rent shall be reduced based on the extent to which the damage interferes with Tenant's reasonable use of Premises. If damage occurs as a result of an act of Tenant or Tenant's guests, only Landlord shall have the right of termination, and no reduction in Rent shall be made.

36. INSURANCE: A. Tenant's or guest's personal property and vehicles are not insured by Landlord, manager or, if applicable, HOA, against loss or damage due to fire, theft, vandalism, rain, water, criminal or negligent acts of others, or any other cause. **Tenant is advised to carry Tenant's own insurance (renter's insurance) to protect Tenant from any such loss or damage. B.** Tenant shall comply with any requirement imposed on Tenant by Landlord's insurer to avoid: **(i)** an increase in Landlord's insurance premium (or Tenant shall pay for the increase in premium); or **(ii)** loss of insurance. **C.** ☐ Tenant shall obtain liability insurance, in an amount not less than $_____, naming Landlord and, if applicable, Property Manager as additional insured for injury or damage to, or upon, the Premises during the term of this agreement or any extension. Tenant shall provide Landlord a copy of the insurance policy before commencement of this Agreement, and a rider prior to any renewal.

37. WATERBEDS/PORTABLE WASHERS: Tenant shall not use or have waterbeds on the Premises unless: **(i)** Tenant obtains a valid waterbed insurance policy; **(ii)** Tenant increases the security deposit in an amount equal to one-half of one month's Rent; and **(iii)** the bed conforms to the floor load capacity of the Premises ☐ Portable Dishwasher; ☐ Portable Washing Machine.

38. WAIVER: The waiver of any breach shall not be construed as a continuing waiver of the same or any subsequent breach.

39. NOTICE: Notices may be served at the following address, or at any other location subsequently designated:
Landlord: Tenant:
ABC Property Management Company   *1234 Sample Street*
                                                Sample, CA 90000

40. TENANT ESTOPPEL CERTIFICATE: Tenant shall execute and return a tenant estoppel certificate delivered to Tenant by Landlord or Landlord's agent within **3 days** after its receipt (C.A.R. Form TEC). Failure to comply with this requirement shall be deemed Tenant's acknowledgment that the tenant estoppel certificate is true and correct, and may be relied upon by a lender or purchaser.

41. REPRESENTATION
    A. TENANT REPRESENTATION; OBLIGATIONS REGARDING OCCUPANTS; CREDIT: Landlord warrants that all statements in Tenant's rental application are accurate. Landlord requires all occupants 18 years of age or older and all emancipated minors to complete a lease rental application. Tenant acknowledges this requirement and agrees to notify Landlord when any occupant of the Premises reaches the age of 18 or becomes an emancipated minor. Tenant authorizes Landlord and Broker(s) to obtain Tenant's credit report periodically during the tenancy in connection with the modification or enforcement of this Agreement. Landlord may cancel this Agreement: **(i)** before occupancy begins; upon disapproval of the credit report(s), or upon discovering that information in Tenant's application is false; **(ii)** After commencement date, upon disapproval of an updated credit report, or upon discovering that information

Tenant's Initials (_____) (_____)   Landlord's Initials (_____) (_____)

LR REVISED 6/17 (PAGE 5 OF 7)
RESIDENTIAL LEASE OR MONTH-TO-MONTH RENTAL AGREEMENT (LR PAGE 5 OF 7)

調停：本契約内容・条項以外でテナントと家主が争う場合、両者は調停に同意

弁護士費用：勝訴者は弁護士費用（1,000ドル未満）を得る。

C.A.R. フォーム：
C.A.R. フォームはテナント、家主両者とも合意。
[C.A.R. は、California Association of Realtors カリフォルニア州不動産業者協会]

その他条件；追加補足：(他に条件などがあれば、記載)

時；契約全体；変更：変更などの追加書類は契約書全体としてみなされる。

代理者：家主、テナント両者の代理業者

テナントからの代理業者への報酬：
テナントが支払う代理業者への報酬があれば、その両者間で契約を締結

通訳者／翻訳者：通訳・翻訳される言語

翻訳の契約書受け取り通知：スペイン語、中国語、韓国語、フィリピン語、ベトナム語で賃貸契約が取引された場合、その外国語で翻訳された契約書のコピーを州法により家主はテナントに渡さなければならない。

家主からの代理業者への報酬：
家主が支払う代理業者への報酬があれば、その両者間で契約を締結

領収書：第5項で示された金額を家主または代理業者は、入居資金として受領

代表権限：当事者の代表として本契約を署名し執行する場合、後の第55項、第56項で述べその書類を付保

第3章
アメリカ不動産と訴訟

Premises: *1234 Sample Street, Sample, CA 90000* Date: **May 15, 2018**

in Tenant's application is no longer true. A negative credit report reflecting on Tenant's record may be submitted to a credit reporting agency if Tenant fails to fulfill the terms of payment and other obligations under this Agreement.

B. LANDLORD REPRESENTATIONS: Landlord warrants that, unless otherwise specified in writing, Landlord is unaware of **(i)** any recorded Notices of Default affecting the Premise, **(ii)** any delinquent amounts due under any loan secured by the Premises; and **(iii)** any bankruptcy proceeding affecting the Premises.

42. **MEDIATION:**
   A. Consistent with paragraphs B and C below, Landlord and Tenant agree to mediate any dispute or claim arising between them out of this Agreement, or any resulting transaction, before resorting to court action. Mediation fees, if any, shall be divided equally among the parties involved. If, for any dispute or claim to which this paragraph applies, any party commences an action without first attempting to resolve the matter through mediation, or refuses to mediate after a request has been made, then that party shall not be entitled to recover attorney fees, even if they would otherwise be available to that party in any such action.
   B. The following matters are excluded from mediation: **(i)** an unlawful detainer action; **(ii)** the filing or enforcement of a mechanic's lien; and **(iii)** any matter within the jurisdiction of a probate, small claims or bankruptcy court. The filing of a court action to enable the recording of a notice of pending action, for order of attachment, receivership, injunction, or other provisional remedies, shall not constitute a waiver of the mediation provision.
   C. Landlord and Tenant agree to mediate disputes or claims involving Listing Agent, Leasing Agent or property manager ("Broker"), provided Broker shall have agreed to such mediation prior to, or within a reasonable time after, the dispute or claim is presented to such Broker. Any election by Broker to participate in mediation shall not result in Broker being deemed a party to this Agreement.

43. **ATTORNEY FEES:** In any action or proceeding arising out of this Agreement, the prevailing party between Landlord and Tenant shall be entitled to reasonable attorney fees and costs, collectively not to exceed $1,000 (or $_____), except as provided in paragraph 42A.

44. **C.A.R. FORM:** C.A.R. Form means the specific form referenced or another comparable form agreed to by the parties.

45. **OTHER TERMS AND CONDITIONS; SUPPLEMENTS:** If checked, the following ATTACHED documents are incorporated in this agreement:
☐ Keysafe/Lockbox Addendum (C.A.R. Form KLA); ☐ Lead-Based Paint and Lead-Based Paint Hazards Disclosure (C.A.R. Form FLD);
☐ Lease/Rental Mold and Ventilation Addendum (C.A.R. Form LRM); ☐ Landlord in Default Addendum (C.A.R. Form LID
Other _____

46. **TIME OF ESSENCE; ENTIRE CONTRACT; CHANGES:** Time is of the essence. All understandings between the parties are incorporated in this Agreement. Its terms are intended by the parties as a final, complete and exclusive expression of their Agreement with respect to its subject matter, and may not be contradicted by evidence of any prior agreement or contemporaneous oral agreement. If any provision of this Agreement is held to be ineffective or invalid, the remaining provisions will nevertheless be given full force and effect. Neither this Agreement nor any provision in it may be extended, amended, modified, altered or changed except in writing. This Agreement is subject to California landlord-tenant law and shall incorporate all changes required by amendment or successors to such law. This Agreement and any supplement, addendum or modification, including any copy, may be signed in two or more counterparts, all of which shall constitute one and the same writing.

47. **AGENCY:**
   A. **CONFIRMATION:** The following agency relationship(s) are hereby confirmed for this transaction:
   Listing Agent: (Print firm name) _____
   is the agent of (check one): ☐ the Landlord exclusively; or ☐ both the Landlord and Tenant.
   Leasing Agent: (Print firm name) _____
   (if not same as Listing Agent) is the agent of (check one): ☐ the Tenant exclusively; or ☐ the Landlord exclusively; or ☐ both the Tenant and Landlord.
   B. **DISCLOSURE:** ☐ (If checked): The term of this Agreement exceeds one year. A disclosure regarding real estate agency relationships (C.A.R. Form AD) has been provided to Landlord and Tenant, who each acknowledge its receipt.

48. ☐ **TENANT COMPENSATION TO BROKER:** Upon execution of this Agreement, Tenant agrees to pay compensation to Broker as specified in a separate written agreement between Tenant and Broker.

49. ☐ **INTERPRETER/TRANSLATOR:** The terms of this Agreement have been interpreted for Tenant into the following language: _____. Landlord and Tenant acknowledge receipt of the attached interpreter/translator agreement (C.A.R. Form ITA).

50. **NOTICE OF RIGHT TO RECEIVE FOREIGN LANGUAGE TRANSLATION OF LEASE/RENTAL AGREEMENTS:** California Civil Code requires a landlord or property manager to provide a tenant with a foreign language translation copy of a lease or rental agreement if the agreement was negotiated primarily in Spanish, Chinese, Korean, Tagalog or Vietnamese. If applicable, every term of the lease/rental needs to be translated except for, among others, names, dollar amounts and dates written as numerals, and words with no generally accepted non-English translation.

51. **OWNER COMPENSATION TO BROKER:** Upon execution of this Agreement, Owner agrees to pay compensation to Broker as specified in a separate written agreement between Owner and Broker (C.A.R. Form LL or LCA).

52. **RECEIPT:** If specified in paragraph 5, Landlord or Broker, acknowledges receipt of move-in funds.

53. **REPRESENTATIVE CAPACITY:** If one or more Parties is signing this Agreement in a representative capacity and not for him/herself as an individual then that Party shall so indicate in paragraph 55 or 56 and attach a Representative Capacity Signature Disclosure (C.A.R. Form RCSD). Wherever the signature or initials of the representative identified in the RCSD appear on this Agreement or any related documents, it shall be deemed to be in a representative capacity for the entity described and not in an individual capacity, unless otherwise indicated. The Party acting in a representative capacity (i) represents that the entity for which that party is acting already exists and (ii) shall Deliver to the other Party and Escrow Holder, within 3 Days After Acceptance, evidence of authority to act in that capacity (such as but not limited to: applicable portion of the trust or Certification Of Trust (Probate Code §18100.5), letters testamentary, court order, power of attorney, corporate resolution, or formation documents of the business entity).

Landlord and Tenant acknowledge and agree Brokers: **(a)** do not guarantee the condition of the Premises; **(b)** cannot verify representations made by others; **(c)** cannot provide legal or tax advice; **(d)** will not provide other advice or information that exceeds the knowledge, education or experience required to obtain a real estate license. Furthermore, if Brokers are not also acting as Landlord in this Agreement, Brokers: **(e)** do not decide what rental rate a Tenant should pay or Landlord should accept; and **(f)** do not decide upon the length or other terms of this Agreement. Landlord and Tenant agree that they will seek legal, tax, insurance and other desired assistance from appropriate professionals.

Tenant's Initials (_____) (_____)   Landlord's Initials (_____) (_____)

LR REVISED 6/17 (PAGE 6 OF 7)
RESIDENTIAL LEASE OR MONTH-TO-MONTH RENTAL AGREEMENT (LR PAGE 6 OF 7)

Produced with zipForm® by zipLogix 18070 Fifteen Mile Road, Fraser, Michigan 48026 www.zipLogix.com   *1234 Sample*

物件管理は家主：(または) 家主代理業者、
またはリーシング業者、または物件管理会社

上記の条件にて本物件を賃借する：
テナント署名 _____
テナント名 _____
住所 _____等

上記の条件にて本物件を賃借する：
家主（または代理業者）_____
家主名 _____
住所 _____等

第3章
アメリカ不動産と訴訟

Premises: *1234 Sample Street, Sample, CA 90000*   Date: **May 15, 2018**

54. The Premises is being managed by Owner, (or, if checked):
☐ Listing firm in box below   ☐ Leasing firm in box below   ☐ Property Management firm immediately below

Real Estate Broker (Property Manager) *ABC Property Management Company*   CalBRE Lic # _____
By (Agent) _____ CalBRE Lic # _____
Address _____ Telephone # _____

55. Tenant agrees to rent the Premises on the above terms and conditions.
☐ One or more Tenants is signing this Agreement in a representative capacity and not for him/herself as an individual. See attached Representative Capacity Signature Disclosure (For Tenant Representative) (C.A.R. Form RCSD-T) for additional terms.

Tenant _____ Date _____
Print Name *John Tenant*
Address _____ City _____ State _____ Zip _____
Telephone _____ Fax _____ E-mail _____
Tenant _____ Date _____
Print Name _____
Address _____ City _____ State _____ Zip _____
Telephone _____ Fax _____ E-mail _____

☐ **GUARANTEE:** In consideration of the execution of this Agreement by and between Landlord and Tenant and for valuable consideration, receipt of which is hereby acknowledged, the undersigned ("Guarantor") does hereby: **(i)** guarantee unconditionally to Landlord and Landlord's agents, successors and assigns, the prompt payment of Rent or other sums that become due pursuant to this Agreement, including any and all court costs and attorney fees included in enforcing the Agreement; **(ii)** consent to any changes, modifications or alterations of any term in this Agreement agreed to by Landlord and Tenant; and **(iii)** waive any right to require Landlord and/or Landlord's agents to proceed against Tenant for any default occurring under this Agreement before seeking to enforce this Guarantee.

Guarantor (Print Name) _____
Guarantor _____ Date _____
Address _____ City _____ State _____ Zip _____
Telephone _____ Fax _____ E-mail _____

56. Landlord (owner or ☐ agent for owner) agrees to rent the Premises on the above terms and conditions.
☐ One or more Landlords is signing this Agreement in a representative capacity and not for him/herself as an individual. See attached Representative Capacity Signature Disclosure (For Landlord Representative) (C.A.R. Form RCSD-LL) for additional terms.

Landlord _____ Date _____ Landlord _____ Date _____
Taro Nippon
Address _____
Telephone _____ Fax _____ E-mail _____

REAL ESTATE BROKERS:
A. Real estate brokers who are not also Landlord under this Agreement are not parties to the Agreement between Landlord and Tenant.
B. Agency relationships are confirmed in paragraph 44.
C. **COOPERATING BROKER COMPENSATION:** Listing Broker agrees to pay Cooperating Broker (Leasing Firm) and Cooperating Broker agrees to accept: **(i)** the amount specified in the MLS, provided Cooperating Broker is a Participant of the MLS in which the Property is offered for sale or lease or a reciprocal MLS; or **(ii)** ☐ (if checked) the amount specified in a separate written agreement between Listing Broker and Cooperating Broker.

Real Estate Broker (Leasing Firm) _____ CalBRE Lic. # _____
By (Agent) _____ CalBRE Lic. # _____ Date _____
Address _____ City _____ State _____ Zip _____
Telephone _____ Fax _____ E-mail _____

Real Estate Broker (Listing Firm) _____ CalBRE Lic. # _____
By (Agent) _____ CalBRE Lic. # _____ Date _____
Address _____ City _____ State _____ Zip _____
Telephone _____ Fax _____ E-mail _____

© 2017, California Association of REALTORS®, Inc. United States copyright law (Title 17 U.S. Code) forbids the unauthorized distribution, display and reproduction of this form, or any portion thereof, by photocopy machine or any other means, including facsimile or computerized formats.
THIS FORM HAS BEEN APPROVED BY THE CALIFORNIA ASSOCIATION OF REALTORS®. NO REPRESENTATION IS MADE AS TO THE LEGAL VALIDITY OR ACCURACY OF ANY PROVISION IN ANY SPECIFIC TRANSACTION. A REAL ESTATE BROKER IS THE PERSON QUALIFIED TO ADVISE ON REAL ESTATE TRANSACTIONS. IF YOU DESIRE LEGAL OR TAX ADVICE, CONSULT AN APPROPRIATE PROFESSIONAL.

Published and Distributed by:
REAL ESTATE BUSINESS SERVICES, INC.
a subsidiary of the California Association of REALTORS®
525 South Virgil Avenue, Los Angeles, California 90020

Reviewed by _____ Date _____

LR REVISED 6/17 (PAGE 7 OF 7)
RESIDENTIAL LEASE OR MONTH-TO-MONTH RENTAL AGREEMENT (LR PAGE 7 OF 7)

Produced with zipForm® by zipLogix 18070 Fifteen Mile Road, Fraser, Michigan 48026 www.zipLogix.com   1234 Sample

BED BUG DISCLOSURE
(C.A.R. Form BBD, 6/17)
(California Civil Code §1954.603)

The following terms and conditions are hereby incorporated in and made a part of the: Residential Lease or Month-to-Month Rental Agreement, ("Agreement"), dated **May 15, 2018**, on property known as **1234 Sample Street, Sample, CA 90000**,

in which **John Tenant** is referred to as ("Tenant")
and **Taro Nippon** is referred to as ("Landlord").

INFORMATION ABOUT BED BUGS:

1. Bed Bug Appearance: Bed bugs have six legs. Adult bed bugs have flat bodies about 1/4 of an inch in length. Their color can vary from red and brown to copper colored. Young bed bugs are very small. Their bodies are about 1/16 of an inch in length. They have almost no color. When a bed bug feeds, its body swells, may lengthen, and becomes bright red, sometimes making it appear to be a different insect. Bed bugs do not fly. They can either crawl or be carried from place to place on objects, people, or animals. Bed bugs can be hard to find and identify because they are tiny and try to stay hidden.
2. Life Cycle and Reproduction: An average bed bug lives for about 10 months. Female bed bugs lay one to five eggs per day. Bed bugs grow to full adulthood in about 21 days.
3. Bed bugs can survive for months without feeding.
4. Bed Bug Bites: Because bed bugs usually feed at night, most people are bitten in their sleep and do not realize they were bitten. A person's reaction to insect bites is an immune response and so varies from person to person. Sometimes the red welts caused by the bites will not be noticed until many days after a person was bitten, if at all.
5. Common signs and symptoms of a possible bed bug infestation:
   A. Small red to reddish brown fecal spots on mattresses, box springs, bed frames, mattresses, linens, upholstery, or walls.
   B. Molted bed bug skins, white, sticky eggs, or empty eggshells.
   C. Very heavily infested areas may have a characteristically sweet odor.
   D. Red, itchy bite marks, especially on the legs, arms, and other body parts exposed while sleeping. However, some people do not show bed bug lesions on their bodies even though bed bugs may have fed on them.
6. For more information, see the Internet Web sites of the United States Environmental Protection Agency and the National Pest Management Association.
7. Tenant shall report suspected infestations by bed bugs to the Landlord or Property Manager at the mailing or email address or phone provided in the Agreement and cooperate with any inspection for and treatment of bed bugs.
8. Landlord will notify tenants of any units inspected by a pest control operator of the findings by such an operator within 2 business days of the receipt of the findings. All Tenants will be notified of confirmed infestations within common areas.

The foregoing terms and conditions are hereby agreed to, and the undersigned acknowledge receipt of a copy of this document.

Date **May**, **2018**   Date **May**, **2018**

Tenant _____   Landlord _____
       John Tenant   **Taro Nippon**
Tenant _____   Landlord _____

© 2017, California Association of REALTORS®, Inc. United States copyright law (Title 17 U.S. Code) forbids the unauthorized distribution, display and reproduction of this form, or any portion thereof, by photocopy machine or any other means, including facsimile or computerized formats.
THIS FORM HAS BEEN APPROVED BY THE CALIFORNIA ASSOCIATION OF REALTORS®. NO REPRESENTATION IS MADE AS TO THE LEGAL VALIDITY OR ACCURACY OF ANY SPECIFIC PROVISION IN ANY SPECIFIC TRANSACTION. A REAL ESTATE BROKER IS THE PERSON QUALIFIED TO ADVISE ON REAL ESTATE TRANSACTIONS. IF YOU DESIRE LEGAL OR TAX ADVICE, CONSULT AN APPROPRIATE PROFESSIONAL.
This form is made available to real estate professionals through an agreement with or purchase from the California Association of REALTORS®. It is not intended to identify the user as a REALTOR®. REALTOR® is a registered collective membership mark which may be used only by members of the NATIONAL ASSOCIATION OF REALTORS® who subscribe to its Code of Ethics.

Published and Distributed by:
REAL ESTATE BUSINESS SERVICES, INC.
a subsidiary of the California Association of REALTORS®
525 South Virgil Avenue, Los Angeles, California 90020

BBD 6/17 (PAGE 1 OF 1)   Reviewed by _____ Date _____

BED BUG DISCLOSURE (BBD PAGE 1 OF 1)

2 保険について

アメリカ不動産投資において、火災保険など物件にかかわる保険は非常に重要です。この保険を理解することは、投資家であれば当然のことになります。つまり、知っていて当然、知らないほうが悪い、損をするということになります。ここでは保険についてさらにくわしく紹介しておきます。

不動産にかかわる保険は、主に次の4つになります。

① **火災保険**
② **損害賠償保険とオーナー保険（HO6）**
③ **地震保険**
④ **賃貸者（テナント）保険**

① 火災保険

これは文字どおり、家屋が火災で焼失したときにおりる保険です。

一般的には再建設する際にかかるコストをカバーする保険です。この再建設コストが計算されます。保険会社である一定の計算になります。居住面積に応じてこの再建設コストが計算されます。ひとつの目安として、1平方フィート当たり＝約0・92ドルで200ドル前後がコストのようです。たとえば2000平方フィート（＝約184㎡）の居住面積の家屋を再建設する場合、40万ドルとなり、この保険金額をカバーする保険料が計算されます。物件がコンドミニアムやタウンハウスの場合、HOAの保険で建物の再建設はカバーされていますが、各戸内はオーナー自身で別のオーナー保険（HO6）でカバーすることになります。

② 損害賠償保険とオーナー保険（HO6）

たとえば、遊びに来ていた友人が建物内、とくに部屋の中でケガをした場合、そのケガの治療費用をカバーする保険です。

「HO6保険」とはHome Owners保険ということで、コンドミニアム・タウンハウスの物件は共益組合費HOAを支払いますが、その中に建物全体外側の保険は入っているのですが、各ユニット内の個人の所有物、たとえばテレビ、冷蔵庫、ソファーなどはカバーさ

第3章
アメリカ不動産と訴訟

れていません。HO6はそのための個人の所有物・賠償をカバーする保険になります。

図表3-2をご覧ください。これは筆者のコンドミニアムのHO6保険です。

まん中囲みの中の3番目に、「COVERAGE C-PERSONAL PROPERTY」とありますが、これは個人の所有物を保証します。家具、電化製品、コンピューター、食器、衣類など、それらの金額を補償金額として設定します。この場合、2万5000ドルまでカバーしています。

その下の「COVERAGE D- LOSS OF USE」。これは、火災などでしばらくの間他の場所に住むことを余儀なくされた場合、その間の宿泊費などをカバーします。また、賃貸の場合は、火災発生からテナント入居までの空室期間もカバーします。

次の「COVERAGE E-PERSONAL LIABILITY」は、第三者に対する賠償金、誰かにケガをさせてしまった際、訴訟の際の法的な費用などをカバーします。

次の「COVERAGE F-MEDICAL PAYMENTS TO OTHERS」は、自分の家に遊びに来ていた友だちが自分の家でケガをしてしまったなど、そんな時には、その医療費をサポートします。

HO6保険はコンドミニアムやタウンハウスで必要になりますが、一軒家やアパートは、火災保険にオーナーの賠償保険が追加することになります。

図表 3-2

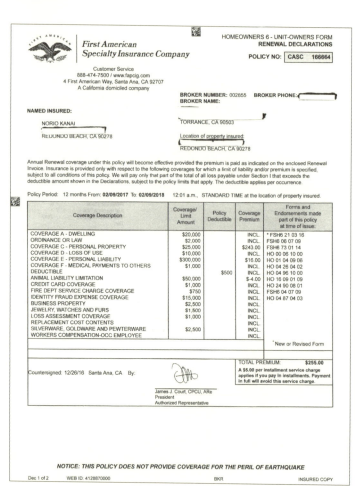

③ 地震保険

地震保険は、前述の保険以外に別途手当てする保険になります。カリフォルニア州は他の州に比べ地震の頻度が比較的多いと思われますので、地震保険に入る方が多いですが、保険料が高いため入らない方もおられます。保険金額等を考慮し検討すべき保険です。California Earthquake Authority の地震保険は比較的安価です。

④ 賃貸者（テナント）保険

これはテナントが自分自身の所有物などをカバーする保険で、賃貸借契約を締結する際に、家主は半強制的にテナントに依頼します。

保険の種類は、取得する物件のタイプにより異なります。

1 コンドミニアムやタウンハウス　HO6
2 一軒家　火災保険、損害賠償保険
3 アパート（集合住宅）　火災保険、損害賠償保険

また保険料は、物件タイプやカバーしたい補償金額によって変わってきますが、基本的には、

A　個人所有の場合、居住面積（Square Footage=s.f.）1s.f.につき40セントが基本料になります。

B　法人所有の場合は、居住面積1s.f.につき50セント以上の基本料に上がります。

たとえば、総居住面積5000平方フィートの集合住宅のアパートを所有している場合、個人所有であれば年間2000ドルから2250ドルですが、法人所有の場合は2500ドル以上になります。とくに非居住者の日本の法人の場合はさらに高くなり、3000ドル程度に上がってしまいます。

これらの金額はあくまで目安で、平均的なStandardの保険料ですが、カバーする補償金額を増やしたい場合は、相当分高くなります。

\こぼれ話 **3** /

人口減少

日本はすでに人口減少が始まっており、しかも少子高齢化であることは衆知のごとくです。そのために社会保障費またその財源などの問題、介護問題、高齢化社会への構造転換、ビジネス・商業形態の変化、生徒数減少による学校存続問題など、あらゆる分野で変化が生じ始めています。不動産もそうで、今後価値が減少したり、地域選別も激化していきます。

このように人口減少は、さまざまな問題を引き起こしていますが、最も大きな問題は国防です。国同士が争ったり戦うことはできる限り避けなければいけませんが、専守防衛も含めて戦わざるを得ないとき、人口の差は、根本的・決定的要因になります。たとえば人口1000万人の国と1万人の国が戦えば、勝負は明らかですね。もちろん最新の技術で最新兵器やロボットで人口数の差を補えば、人口数の差が決定的要因にはなり得ないかもしれませんが、絶対数の違いは大きなかつ基本的要因です。

アメリカの学者の中には、「日本は人口減少問題が大きな問題であるということを自覚していない」と述べている人たちがいます。国家の力・原動力になる人口が少なくなるということは、国家の大事にかかわることで、経済や国防など国の根幹である

部分が弱まるということだそうです。人が少なくなれば、どんどん力が弱まっていきます。国や政府をはじめ、皆で真剣に考え対策を講じていかなくてはなりません。筆者はこの人口減少問題は、いずれボディブローのように後になって効いてくると確信しております。

実は人口減少は日本だけでなく、中国も高齢者社会になっていくといわれていまして、ほぼすべての世界人口はやがて減少に転じ始めるそうです。スーパー老人大国が日本でそれに続くのが中国だそうです。明らかに今までのような社会政策では対応しきれないということで、人生100年時代を迎え、高齢者でも仕事ができる社会環境を整えていくことが重要でしょう。すでにアメリカやヨーロッパの国々では、高齢者が働き続けられる職場作りが始まっています。

そのなかで、先進国というよりもナンバーワンの国アメリカは、人口が増え続けていきます。それはとくに重要な生産者人口の層が増えるそうで、これは国の経済面が増強していくことにほかなりません。

第4章

アメリカ不動産の建物に対する考え方

1 土地より建物比率が高いアメリカ不動産

日本の不動産は建物に比べ土地の価値・割合が高いのですが、アメリカの場合は土地よりも建物比率が高いと一般的にいわれており、アメリカの不動産を取り扱う業者も同じことを言っています。

確かにほとんどの場所ではそのとおりなのですが、ロケーションの良い物件は必ずしもそうではありません。アメリカでも、ビバリーヒルズのような一等地、ニューヨークの摩天楼街、海が全貌できる高級コンドミニアムなど、限られたところの土地の価値は、アメリカでも建物比率よりも土地の価値・比率が高いのが普通です。

アメリカの不動産の土地と建物の価値を決めるのは、物件所在地の郡当局です。郡というのは、いくつかの市をまとめて管轄している役所です。実は当局の最大で唯一の関心事は、物件の価値（売買価格）そのものなのです。理由は簡単で、固定資産税に当たる不動産税（Property Tax）は売買価格をベースに一定の決まった税率で算出します。

第4章
アメリカ不動産の建物に対する考え方

たとえばロサンゼルス郡は、おおむね1.1％〜1.25％で、50万ドルで売買された物件の不動産税は、5500ドル（＝50万ドル×1.1％）から6350ドル（＝50万ドル×1.25％）になります。つまり、税収確保です。

50万ドルの土地と建物の内訳は、税収には全く影響しません。とはいうものの、物件が売買されるたびにその内訳は算出されますが、ロサンゼルス郡の場合、一定の決まりがないように見受けられます。おそらく近隣の直近売買事例をベースに決めているようです。

ちなみにハワイのホノルル郡では、毎年10月1日に不動産税が見直されますので、その際に一緒に土地と建物の割合も見直されるようです。ワシントン州のシアトル市やカリフォルニア州のサンディエゴ郡は、当局に相談できます。当局にAssessorまたはAppraiserという物件評価担当者がいて、その方が相談にのってくれます。

一度ロサンゼルス郡の当局にも問い合わせましたが、土地と建物比率では問い合わせ相談がかなわず、固定資産税の見直しだけになっているようでした。

実は、とても理解不能というか不可解なことがあります。それは、全く同じ居住面積、同じ部屋数、同じフロアープラン、同じ階にあるコンドミニアム（マンション）の建物比率が全く違うのです。ロサンゼルスの当局への問い合わせもこの同じ疑問でしたが、取り合ってもらえませんでした。一般にコンドミニアムやタウンハウス（メゾネット式住宅）は、ほとんどの場合自宅用ですので、減価償却できません。したがいまして、全体の価値

が重要で、その価値で固定資産税が決定されますので、建物比率には無関心なのです。し かしながら、投資目的で所有・運用していれば、建物比率が高いほうが減価償却が増えま すので、全く同じコンドミニアムを購入しても建物比率が低いと合点がいきません。

次に掲げられている図表をご覧ください。図表4－1は、筆者所有の1LDKのコンド ミニアムのロサンゼルス郡当局の固定資産税請求書で、次の図表4－2と図表4－3の2 つが、筆者所有のコンドミニアムと同じところの他の1LDK物件のプロフィールです。 それぞれの中ほどの下のところに、「Improvement」という項目がありますが、これが建 物比率のことになります。筆者の建物比率は72・2％である一方、もうひとつ別の1LD Kの比率は48・6％になっています。全く同じ居住面積、フロアープラン、部屋数、同じ 築年です。これは何も筆者所有のコンドミニアム物件だけでなく、すべてのコンドミニア ムやタウンハウス、アパートの集合住宅に至るまで、建物比率が全く違うのです。

では、賢明なアメリカ人投資家はどうしているのかといいますと、鑑定評価を取ってそ のなかで土地と建物の価値・割合を算出するようにしています。実はこれは確定申告をす る税理士・会計士がアドバイスしているところで、税理士・会計士は当局の査定を全く信 用していませんので、鑑定評価を取るように助言しているのです。それは土地と建物の鑑定評価をする鑑定士 実はもうひとつやっかいな問題があります。

第4章
アメリカ不動産の建物に対する考え方

図表4-1　固定資産税請求書

図表4-2 1LDK物件のプロフィール

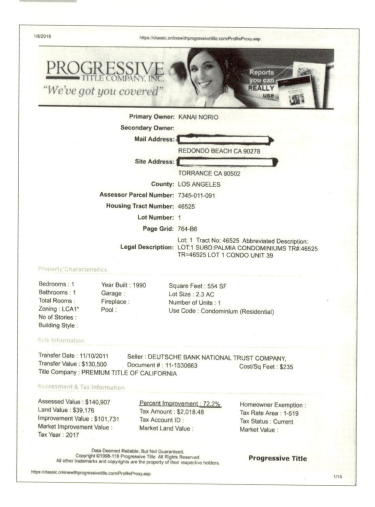

第4章
アメリカ不動産の建物に対する考え方

図表4-3　1LDK物件のプロフィール

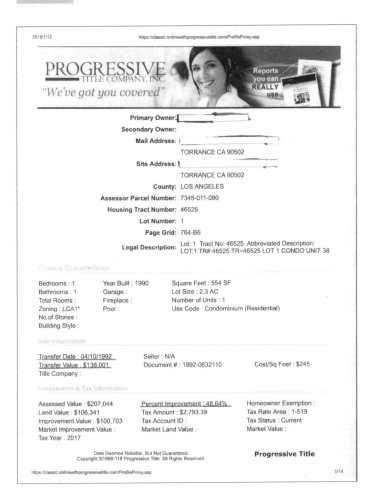

があまりいないということです。筆者はたくさんの鑑定士に問い合わせたとろ、やっと13人目に引き受けてもらうことになりました。

とくにここで申し上げたいのは、アパートのような大型物件になりますと、商業物件専門取扱業者が自分たちの息のかかったところに「Cost Segregation」という手法でかなり高額な料金で受け付けるところがあるようです。注意が必要です。

ここで固定資産税に当たる不動産税 Property Tax について少し説明致します。

ロサンゼルス郡の Property Tax 年度は、7月1日から翌年の6月30日までになります。不動産税の支払期日は年2回で、1回目が11月1日、2回目が翌年の2月1日ですが、それぞれ郵便消印日が12月10日、4月10日が最終日になります。

次に物件売買があった場合の売主と買手の Property Tax はどのように計算されるのかを説明しておきます。

たとえば5月1日に売買が完了したとします。Property Tax の年度は7月1日から翌年6月30日までですので、前の年の7月1日から売買完了日の前日までが売主負担で、5月1日から6月30日までが買手負担になります。5月1日ということは、第2回目支払い期日の2月1日（または4月10日消印）は過ぎていますので、売主は6月30日までの分は支払っていますので、5月1日から6月30日までの分がエスクローで払い戻しされます。

第4章 アメリカ不動産の建物に対する考え方

そこで、売主のProperty Tax額と買手のTax額は異なります。売主のProperty Taxは、売主が同物件を購入した金額、仮に35万ドルで5年前に購入したとします。Property Taxは年間3％程度で増えていきます。具体的な例としまして筆者の先ほどの1LDKのコンドミニアムですが、過去2年間の上昇率は1.52％、2.0％となっています。仮にProperty Taxの税率が1.2％とします。35万ドルで購入したので、購入時の年間Tax額は、35万ドル×1.2％で4200ドルになり、年間4％ずつ上昇するとします。5年後は税率がだいたい1.4％ぐらいになりまして、5年後の税金額は約4900ドル約817ドル（＝4900ドル÷12か月×2か月）が売主にエスクローから戻ってきます。になります。5月1日から6月30日までの2か月間のProperty Taxは戻ってきますので、

買手のほうは、仮に同物件を50万ドルで買い入れるとしますと、Property Taxは6000ドル（＝50万ドル×1.2％）になりますが、とりあえず6月30日までのProperty Tax、817ドルをエスクローを通して支払います。ところが817ドルというのは、4900ドルをベースにしていますので、新しい価格50万ドルベースのProperty Tax、6000ドルで計算し直した2か月分1000ドルになって、この1000ドルとエスクローで支払った2か月分の817ドルの差額183ドルがSupplemental Taxとして後日請求されます。

2 長い耐久年数

アメリカの不動産・建物は、日本の不動産と比較にならないほど、耐久・耐用年数が長いのが特長です。たとえば有名なビバリーヒルズの豪邸の多くは、築50年以上はざらにあります。なかには100年近いものもあります。したがいましてアメリカでは、50年物だから投資対象にはならない、というような概念はなくして考えるべきです。日本とアメリカの不動産の一般的な耐久年数は、次のとおりです。

日本　35年　　アメリカ　100年

建物の諸年数は、**図表4−5**をご覧ください。

とくに気候が温暖なカリフォルニアの不動産の耐用年数は、さらに長くなります。年数が長いので古くなったところは、もちろん改装・改築をして対応します。一般的には内部

第4章
アメリカ不動産の建物に対する考え方

図表 4-5 建物の諸年数

	除去耐用年数	代替わり周期	投資周期
日本	40年	30年	39年
アメリカ	100年	103年	23年

出典:財団法人・日本建築学会

のキッチンやバスルーム、フロアリングなどを、最新の原材料・デザインで改装し、市場レベルよりも高く売却することも可能です。

アメリカ西海岸の物件は、年を通して1年中温暖な気候のため、木造ながら建物耐久年数が長く、老朽化する年数は120年から150年になります。

次ページの写真をご覧ください。

この写真の物件は、有名なビバリーヒルズの住宅ですが、築何年と思いますか? 1927年に建てられた物件ですが、91年前の物件にみえますでしょうか? もちろんリフォームしていますが、91年前に建てられた物件にはとてもみえません。

| 第4章
| アメリカ不動産の建物に対する考え方

第4章
アメリカ不動産の建物に対する考え方

こぼれ話 4

ブランド志向の日本

日本とアメリカの相違点はいろいろありますが、総じて日本（人）は外見、見た目などを気にしますが、アメリカ（人）は中身、実態を重要視します。もちろん例外はありますが……。

とくに日本人は、ブランド名を気にします。ブランド物を持っていると安心するというか、優越感を味わえるとか、一種の保険のようなものです。

財閥系や一部上場大手ゼネコン、建設会社、不動産会社が建てた住宅・マンションだから大丈夫、安心できると信じていたのに、建物が傾いているという問題がありました。大手ゼネコンが建設していれば、耐震、資材、建設規定、消火規制などすべてクリアーしていると自信があるのでしょうか？　手抜き工事は絶対ないと言えるでしょうか？　ご存知のように実際に工事・建設するのは大手ゼネコン・不動産会社ではなく、その下請け業者です。なかにはそのまた下請け業者の孫受け業者の場合もあります。もちろん設計や現場監督はしているはずですが、実際にはどこまで完璧に実施しているのでしょうか？　気を許していれば、手抜き工事があってもおかしくないです。

自動車などの検査段階で検査ライセンスのない人たちに検査させてそれでよしとしていた一部上場企業が摘発されました。

これらは会社の名前、ブランド名を信じているからこそ発生した事件です。日本(人)ならではの出来事です。

これがアメリカではあまり起こりえません。アメリカ(人)は、物事の実態なりを重要視するからです。きちんとチェックします。取り扱う企業が有名で大きい会社だから安心することはなく、中小企業でもきちんと中身を調べて判断します。あるいは、信頼できる友人や仲間からの紹介を受けます。そのほうが会社名より安心するのです。

要するに、物事の本質や本物を見極めるために勉強することです。

第5章

所有権

1 譲渡証書

アメリカの不動産物件の所有権は、タイトル保険で保護され、日本の権利書に当たる書類は、アメリカには存在しません。強いて言えば、物件所在地の郡当局で所有権の移転・譲渡証書を登録・登記する際に、当局の受領印を押した譲渡証書の控えがそうですが、それも正確には、受け付けましたという確認書に過ぎず、権利書ではありません。

また物件を売却する際に、その受領印がある受領書を求められません。では本人の所有権はどうやって証明されるかといいますと、当局に登録・記録されているかどうかということで、これを保険でカバーしているタイトル会社が証明することになります。実は、タイトル保険会社は各登録局のデータをすべて保有しています。同じシステムで同じ情報を共有しているということで、そのなかで記録をチェックして、問題なければ保険を出すという形です。したがって、タイトル保険会社が保険を出すということは、問題ないと判断したからで、それで安心できるのです。

第5章 所有権

実際に登録局が受領し受領印を押した譲渡証書をみてみましょう。**図表5−1をご覧ください**。これは筆者が自宅を購入したときの売主の譲渡証書です。2ページ目をご覧ください。まん中あたりに次の記述があります。

Anastasi Development Company, LLC, a California Limited Liability Company hereby GRANT(S) to Norio Kanai the following described real property in the County of Los Angeles, State of California: Legal description per Exhibit A attached hereto and made a part hereof Commonly known as: Redondo Beach,CA. 90278

「Anastasi Development Company」が売主オーナーで、筆者（Norio Kanai）に下記の物件を「Grant」つまり譲渡する、とうたわれています。

3ページ目に売主代表が公証人（Sharon H. Ruiz）の面前で署名しています。
4ページ目と5ページ目が物件の正式な表記になります。
5ページ目の最後に、次の記述があります。

Assessor's Parcel Number: 4082-012-030

（123ページに続く）

図表 5-1 譲渡証書

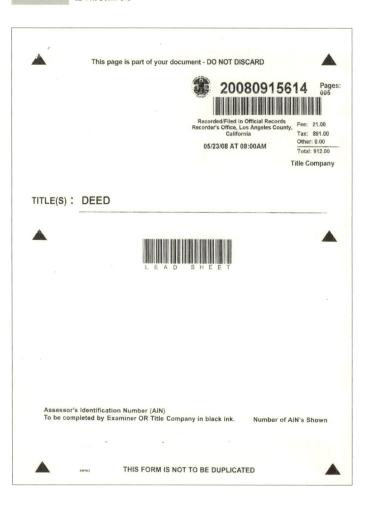

第5章
所有権

RECORDING REQUESTED BY:
LAND LAWYERS TITLE CO.
Order No. 2213862-36
Escrow No. 19608KH
Parcel No. 4082-012-030

AND WHEN RECORDED MAIL TO:

NORIO KANAI

REDONDO BEACH, CA 90278

05/23/08

20080915614

SPACE ABOVE THIS LINE FOR RECORDER'S USE

GRANT DEED

THE UNDERSIGNED GRANTOR(S) DECLARE(S) THAT DOCUMENTARY TRANSFER TAX IS **$297.00** and CITY **$594.00**
- ☒ computed on full value of property conveyed, or
- ☐ computed on full value less liens or encumbrances remaining at the time of sale.
- ☐ unincorporated area: ☒ **Redondo Beach**, and

FOR A VALUABLE CONSIDERATION, receipt of which is hereby acknowledge

Anastasi Development Company, LLC, a California Limited Liability Company

hereby GRANT(S) to   Norio Kanai

the following described real property in the County of **Los Angeles**, State of California:

Legal description per Exhibit A attached hereto and made a part hereof

Commonly known as: ⎡   ⎤ Redondo Beach, CA. 90278

"This deed is made, accepted and subject to any and all matters of record, including taxes, assessments, easements, oil and mineral reservations and leases, if any, rights of way, covenants and agreements and conditions, covenants and restrictions including that certain "Declaration of Covenants, Conditions and Restrictions" recorded **January 11, 2008** as Instrument No. **08-63812** Official Records of said County (the "Declaration"). Said Declaration is hereby incorporated by reference into the body of this instrument the same as though fully set forth herein."

Notice: "California law establishes procedures that must be followed prior to the filing of any action related to a claimed construction defect. These procedures impact the legal rights of a homeowner. These procedures may be found in Title 7 of Part 2 of Division 2 of the California Civil Code commencing with SS895".

SIGNATURE AND NOTARY ACKNOWLEDGEMENT ATTACHED HERETO AND MADE A PART HEREOF

Mail Tax Statement to: SAME AS ABOVE or Address Noted Below

Date April 22, 2008

Anastasi Development Company, LLC, A California
Limited Liability Company

Wayne G. Anast (signature)
By: Wayne G. Anastasi, Managing Member

STATE OF CALIFORNIA }
COUNTY OF Los Angeles } S.S.

On ____4/29/08____, before me, Sharon H. Ruiz _____,
a notary public in and for said State, personally appeared Wayne G. Anastasi who proved to me on the basis of satisfactory evidence to be the person(s) whose name(s) is/are subscribed to the within instrument and acknowledged to me that he/she/they executed the same in his/her/their authorized capacity(ies), and that by his/her/their signature(s) on the instrument the person(s), or the entity upon behalf of which the person(s) acted, executed the instrument.

I certify under PENALTY OF PERJURY under the laws of the State of California that the foregoing paragraph is true and correct.

WITNESS my hand and official seal.

Signature _Sharon H. Ruiz_ (Seal)

SHARON H. RUIZ
Commission # 1550840
Notary Public - California
Los Angeles County
My Comm. Expires Mar 4, 2009

File No: 02213862

4

EXHIBIT "A"

All that certain real property situated in the County of Los Angeles, State of California, described as follows:

A CONDOMINIUM COMPOSED OF:

PARCEL 1:

THAT PORTION OF LOT 1 OF TRACT NO. 60638, IN THE CITY OF REDONDO BEACH, IN THE COUNTY OF LOS ANGELES, STATE OF CALIFORNIA, AS PER MAP RECORDED IN BOOK 1328, PAGE(S) 44 AND 45 OF MAPS, DEFINED AS UNIT OF MODULE 1 ON THAT CERTAIN CONDOMINIUM PLAN ("PLAN") RECORDED ON JANUARY 11, 2008, AS INSTRUMENT NO. 08-63811, IN THE OFFICE OF THE COUNTY RECORDER OF SAID COUNTY.

PARCEL 2:

AN UNDIVIDED 1/48TH FEE SIMPLE INTEREST AS TENANT IN COMMON IN AND TO THE COMMON AREA OF MODULE 1 ON LOT 1 OF TRACT NO. 60638, AS MORE PARTICULARLY DESCRIBED AND DELINEATED ON THE CONDOMINIUM PLAN REFERRED TO ABOVE.

EXCEPT THEREFROM UNITS 102 THROUGH 115,INCLUSIVE, 201 THROUGH 215, 219, 220 AND 301 THROUGH 315, INCLUSIVE, 319 AND 320, AS DEFINED AND DELINEATED ON A CONDOMINIUM PLAN RECORDED JANUARY 11, 2008, AS INSTRUMENT NO. 08-63811, OF OFFICIAL RECORDS.

ALSO EXCEPT THEREFROM, ALL MINERALS, OILS, GASES AND OTHER HYDROCARBONS BY WHATSOEVER NAME KNOWN THAT MAY BE WITHIN OR UNDER SAID PORTION OF SAID LAND, WITHOUT, HOWEVER, THE RIGHT TO DRILL, DIG OR MINE THROUGH THE SURFACE THEREOF, AS EXCEPTED IN THE DEED FROM THE STATE OF CALIFORNIA, RECORDED ON FEBRUARY 28, 1968, AS DOCUMENT NO. 2480 IN BOOK D-3925, PAGE 100, OFFICIAL RECORDS, IN SAID OFFICE OF THE COUNTY RECORDER

RESERVING THEREFROM, AN EXCLUSIVE EASEMENT, FOR ALL USES AND PURPOSES OF A BALCONY AREA AND/OR DECK AREA, TOGETHER WITH THE RIGHT TO GRANT TO OTHERS, OVER AND ACROSS THOSE PORTIONS OF LOT 1 OF TRACT 60638, SHOWN AND DEFINED AS "EXCLUSIVE USE COMMON AREA", ON THE ABOVE REFERRED TO CONDOMINIUM PLAN.

RESERVING THEREFROM, AN EXCLUSIVE EASEMENT FOR ALL USES AND PURPOSES OF A PARKING SPACE AREA TOGETHER WITH THE RIGHT TO GRANT TO OTHERS, OVER AND ACROSS THOSE PORTIONS OF SAID LAND DEFINED AND DELINEATED AS P-1 THROUGH P-191 ON THE ABOVE REFERRED TO CONDOMINIUM PLAN.

ALSO RESERVING THEREFROM, FOR THE BENEFIT OF GRANTOR, ITS SUCCESSORS IN INTEREST AND OTHERS, EASEMENTS FOR ACCESS, USE, ENJOYMENT, CONSTRUCTION, REPAIRS, DRAINAGE AND FOR OTHER PURPOSES, ALL AS MORE FULLY DESCRIBED IN THE DECLARATION OF COVENANTS, CONDITIONS AND RESTRICTIONS FOR BREAKWATER VILLAGE HOMEOWNERS ASSOCIATION, RECORDED ON JANUARY 11, 2008, AS INSTRUMENT NO. 08-63812, OFFICIAL RECORDS AND ALL AMENDMENTS AND SUPPLEMENTS THERETO.

File No: 02213862

PARCEL 3:

AN EXCLUSIVE EASEMENT, APPURTENANT TO PARCEL 1 ABOVE, FOR ALL USES AND PURPOSES OF A BALCONY AREA AND/OR DECK AREA OVER AND ACROSS THAT PORTION OF THE COMMON AREA WITHIN MODULE 1 OF LOT 1 OF SAID TRACT NO. 60638, DEFINED AND DELINEATED AS EXCLUSIVE USE COMMON AREA, WHICH BEARS THE SAME NUMBER AS TO THE UNIT REFERRED TO IN PARCEL 1 ABOVE FOLLOWED BY THE LETTER "Y" ON THE ABOVE REFERENCED CONDOMINIUM PLAN.

PARCEL 4:

AN EXCLUSIVE EASEMENT, APPURTENANT TO PARCEL 1 ABOVE, FOR ALL USES AND PURPOSES OF A PARKING SPACE AREA OVER AND ACROSS THAT PORTION OF THE COMMON AREA WITHIN MODULE 1 OF LOT 1 OF SAID TRACT NO. 60638, DEFINED AND DELINEATED AS EXCLUSIVE USE COMMON AREA, ON THE CONDOMINIUM PLAN REFERRED TO IN PARCEL 1 ABOVE FOLLOWED BY THE LETTER "P-106".

Assessor's Parcel Number: **4082-012-030**

(117ページから続く)

この番号が物件の登録局の番号で正式な番号になり、この番号で登録上の物件が決定しますので、物件購入の際などにはこの番号を正確に確認することが肝要になります。

1ページ目をご覧ください。右上のほうに次の記述があります。

Recorded/Filed in Official Records
Recorder's office, Los Angeles County, California
05/23/08 AT 08:00AM

これは「この譲渡証書はロサンゼルス郡の登録局に2008年5月23日午前8時に登録・記録された」と書かれています。これで登録されたことになります。

2 タイトル・レポート

前述しましたが、この受領書は権利書ではありません。タイトル保険会社が「タイトル・レポート」という書類を用意します。物件を売却する時にこの受領書は必要ありません。

図表5-2が筆者の賃貸物件1LDKのコンドミニアムのレポートです。もし筆者がこの物件を売却しようとしたとき、筆者が当該物件のオーナーであるかどうかなどは、このタイトルレポートでチェックします。

2ページ目をご覧ください。「Schedule A」というページで、上から5行目に本物件のタイトル（所有権）は、次の6行目、「Norio Kanai」にある、と書かれています。これで物件の所有者を正式に確認することができます。

3ページ目の「Exhibit "A"」には、正式な物件の法的所在地が記載されています。

その次の4ページ目と5ページ目にはSchedule Bとして、固定資産税の状況、各種先

（130ページに続く）

第5章
所有権

図表 5-2 タイトル・レポート

PROGRESSIVE TITLE COMPANY
801 NORTH BRAND BLVD. SUITE 400
GLENDALE, CA 91203
PHONE: (800) 311-4549
FAX: (818) 550-0532

DATED AS OF FEBRUARY 12, 2018 AT 7:30 A.M.

YOUR NO.:
PROPERTY ADDRESS:
TORRANCE AREA, CA

ORDER NO.: PR1810221
TITLE OFFICER: DANIELLE KENNEY
EMAIL:
GLENDALEUNIT10@PROGRESSIVETITLE.COM

"PRELIMINARY REPORT"

IN RESPONSE TO THE ABOVE REFERENCED APPLICATION FOR A POLICY OF TITLE INSURANCE, **PROGRESSIVE TITLE COMPANY** HEREBY REPORTS THAT IT IS PREPARED TO ISSUE, OR CAUSE TO BE ISSUED, AS OF THE DATE HEREOF, A POLICY OR POLICIES OF TITLE INSURANCE DESCRIBING THE LAND AND THE ESTATE OR INTEREST THEREIN HEREINAFTER SET FORTH, INSURING AGAINST LOSS WHICH MAY BE SUSTAINED BY REASON OF ANY DEFECT, LIEN OR ENCUMBRANCE NOT SHOWN OR REFERRED TO AS AN EXCEPTION BELOW OR NOT EXCLUDED FROM COVERAGE PURSUANT TO THE PRINTED SCHEDULES, CONDITIONS AND STIPULATIONS OF SAID POLICY FORMS.

THE PRINTED EXCEPTIONS AND EXCLUSIONS FROM THE COVERAGE OF SAID POLICY OR POLICIES ARE SET FORTH IN EXHIBIT B ATTACHED. THE POLICY TO BE ISSUED MAY CONTAIN AN ARBITRATION CLAUSE. WHEN THE AMOUNT OF INSURANCE IS LESS THAN THAT SET FORTH IN THE ARBITRATION CLAUSE, ALL ARBITRABLE MATTERS SHALL BE ARBITRATED AT THE OPTION OF EITHER THE COMPANY OR THE INSURED AS THE EXCLUSIVE REMEDY OF THE PARTIES. LIMITATIONS ON COVERED RISKS APPLICABLE TO THE CLTA AND ALTA HOMEOWNER'S POLICIES OF TITLE INSURANCE WHICH ESTABLISH A DEDUCTIBLE AMOUNT AND A MAXIMUM DOLLAR LIMIT OF LIABILITY FOR CERTAIN COVERAGES ARE SET FORTH IN THE POLICY. COPIES OF THE POLICY FORMS SHOULD BE READ. THEY ARE AVAILABLE FROM THE OFFICE THAT ISSUED THIS REPORT.

PLEASE READ THE EXCEPTIONS SHOWN OR REFERRED TO BELOW AND THE EXCEPTIONS AND EXCLUSIONS SET FORTH IN EXHIBIT B OF THIS REPORT CAREFULLY. THE EXCEPTIONS AND EXCLUSIONS ARE MEANT TO PROVIDE YOU WITH NOTICE OF MATTERS WHICH ARE NOT COVERED UNDER THE TERMS OF THE TITLE INSURANCE POLICY AND SHOULD BE CAREFULLY CONSIDERED.

IT IS IMPORTANT TO NOTE THAT THIS PRELIMINARY REPORT IS NOT A WRITTEN REPRESENTATION AS TO THE CONDITION OF TITLE AND MAY NOT LIST ALL LIENS, DEFECTS AND ENCUMBRANCES AFFECTING TITLE TO THE LAND.

THIS REPORT (AND ANY SUPPLEMENTS OR AMENDMENTS HERETO) IS ISSUED SOLELY FOR THE PURPOSE OF FACILITATING THE ISSUANCE OF A POLICY OF TITLE INSURANCE AND NO LIABILITY IS ASSUMED HEREBY. IF IT IS DESIRED THAT LIABILITY BE ASSUMED PRIOR TO THE ISSUANCE OF A POLICY OF TITLE INSURANCE, A BINDER OR COMMITMENT SHOULD BE REQUESTED.

THE FORM OF POLICY OF TITLE INSURANCE CONTEMPLATED BY THIS REPORT IS:

AMERICAN LAND TITLE ASSOCIATION SHORT FORM RESIDENTIAL LOAN POLICY

ORDER NO. PR1810221

SCHEDULE A

THE ESTATE OR INTEREST IN THE LAND HEREINAFTER DESCRIBED OR REFERRED TO COVERED BY THIS REPORT IS:

A CONDOMINIUM AS DEFINED IN SECTION 783 OF THE CALIFORNIA CIVIL CODE, IN FEE AS TO PARCEL 1; AN EASEMENT AS TO PARCEL 2 AND 3.

TITLE TO SAID ESTATE OR INTEREST AT THE DATE HEREOF IS VESTED IN:

NORIO KANAI, ██████████████████████████ **PROPERTY**

THE LAND REFERRED TO IN THIS REPORT IS SITUATED IN THE COUNTY OF LOS ANGELES, STATE OF CALIFORNIA AND IS DESCRIBED AS FOLLOWS:

SEE EXHIBIT "A" ATTACHED HERETO

ORDER NO. PR1810221

EXHIBIT "A"

A CONDOMINIUM COMPRISED OF:

PARCEL 1:

(A) AN UNDIVIDED 1/66TH INTEREST IN AND TO LOT 1 OF TRACT NO. 46525, IN THE COUNTY OF LOS ANGELES, STATE OF CALIFORNIA, AS PER MAP RECORDED IN BOOK 1165 PAGE(S) 9 AND 10 INCLUSIVE OF MAPS, IN THE OFFICE OF THE COUNTY RECORDER OF SAID COUNTY.

EXCEPT THEREFROM UNITS 1 THROUGH 66 INCLUSIVE, AS DEFINED AND DELINEATED ON A CONDOMINIUM PLAN RECORDED AUGUST 26, 1991 AS INSTRUMENT NO. 91-1336563, OFFICIAL RECORDS.

(B) UNIT ☐ AS DEFINED AND DELINEATED ON THE ABOVE REFERENCED TO CONDOMINIUM PLAN.

PARCEL 2:

AN EXCLUSIVE EASEMENT, APPURTENANT TO PARCEL 1 ABOVE, FOR ALL USES AND PURPOSES OF A "DECK AREA" OVER AND ACROSS THAT PORTION OF LOT 1 OF TRACT NO. 46525, DEFINED AND DELINEATED AS "EXCLUSIVE USE AREA" WHICH BEARS THE SAME NUMBER AS THE UNIT REFERRED TO IN PARCEL 1 ABOVE FOLLOWED B THE LETTER "(39-D)" ON THE ABOVE REFERENCED CONDOMINIUM PLAN.

PARCEL 3:

AN EXCLUSIVE EASEMENT, APPURTENANT TO PARCEL 1 ABOVE, FOR ALL USES AND PURPOSES OF A "GARAGE SPACE" OVER AND ACROSS THAT PORTIONS OF LOT 1 OF TRACT NO. 46525, DEFINED AND DELINEATED AS "EXCLUSIVE USE AREA" (72-G), WHICH HAS BEEN ASSIGNED AS SHOWN ON SHEET 5 OF THE ABOVE REFERENCED CONDOMINIUM PLAN.

ORDER NO. PR1810221

SCHEDULE B

AT THE DATE HEREOF EXCEPTIONS TO COVERAGE IN ADDITION TO THE PRINTED EXCEPTIONS AND EXCLUSIONS IN SAID POLICY FORM DESIGNATED ON THE FACE PAGE OF THIS REPORT WOULD BE AS FOLLOWS:

A. GENERAL AND SPECIAL TAXES FOR THE FISCAL YEAR 2018-2019, A LIEN NOT YET DUE OR PAYABLE.

B. GENERAL AND SPECIAL TAXES FOR THE FISCAL YEAR 2017-2018

TOTAL:	$2,018.48
FIRST INSTALLMENT:	$1,009.24, PAID
SECOND INSTALLMENT:	$1,009.24, OPEN
ASSESSED VALUATION:	
LAND VALUE:	$39,176.00
IMPROVEMENT VALUE:	$101,731.00
EXEMPTIONS:	NONE
CODE AREA:	01519
A. P. NO.:	7345-011-091

C. THE LIEN OF SUPPLEMENTAL TAXES ASSESSED PURSUANT TO CHAPTER 3.5 COMMENCING WITH SECTION 75 OF THE CALIFORNIA REVENUE AND TAXATION CODE.

1. COVENANTS, CONDITIONS AND RESTRICTIONS, IF ANY, APPEARING IN THE PUBLIC RECORDS, BUT DELETING ANY COVENANT, CONDITION OR RESTRICTION INDICATING A PREFERENCE, LIMITATION, OR DISCRIMINATION BASED ON RACE, COLOR, RELIGION, SEX, GENDER, GENDER IDENTITY, GENDER EXPRESSION, SEXUAL ORIENTATION, FAMILIAL STATUS, MARITAL STATUS, DISABILITY, GENETIC INFORMATION, NATIONAL ORIGIN, SOURCE OF INCOME, OR ANCESTRY, TO THE EXTENT THAT SUCH COVENANTS, CONDITIONS, OR RESTRICTIONS VIOLATES TITLE 42, SECTION 3604(C), OF THE UNITED STATES CODES OR SECTION 12955 OF THE CALIFORNIA GOVERNMENT CODE, OR CALIFORNIA ASSEMBLY BILL 887. LAWFUL RESTRICTIONS UNDER STATE AND FEDERAL LAW ON THE AGE OF OCCUPANTS IN SENIOR HOUSING OR HOUSING FOR OLDER PERSONS SHALL NOT BE CONSTRUED AS RESTRICTIONS BASED ON FAMILIAL STATUS.

2. ANY EASEMENTS OR SERVITUDES APPEARING IN THE PUBLIC RECORDS.

3. ANY LEASE, GRANT, EXCEPTION OR RESERVATION OF MINERALS OR MINERAL RIGHTS APPEARING IN THE PUBLIC RECORDS.

4. **OUR EXAMINATION OF RECORD TITLE TO THE HEREIN DESCRIBED LAND DOES NOT DISCLOSE ANY EXISTING LOANS. WE THEREFORE REQUIRE THE OWNERS DECLARATION ATTACHED HERETO BE SIGNED, NOTARIZED, AND RETURNED TO US BEFORE RECORDING.**

5. ANY DEFECTS, LIENS, ENCUMBRANCES OR OTHER MATTERS WHICH NAME PARTIES WITH THE SAME OR SIMILAR NAMES AS THE VESTEE(S).

ORDER NO. PR1810221

REQUIREMENTS:

6. PRIOR TO THE ISSUANCE OF ANY POLICY OF TITLE INSURANCE, THE COMPANY WILL REQUIRE:

A. THE NAME SEARCH NECESSARY TO ASCERTAIN THE EXISTENCE OF MATTERS REFERRED TO IN ITEM NO. 5 HAS NOT BEEN COMPLETED. IN ORDER TO COMPLETE THIS PRELIMINARY REPORT OR COMMITMENT, WE WILL REQUIRE A STATEMENT OF INFORMATION.

IMPORTANT: PLEASE FORWARD THE STATEMENT OF INFORMATION TO US <u>AS SOON AS POSSIBLE</u>, BUT <u>NO LATER THAN 10 WORKING DAYS BEFORE CLOSING</u>. THIS WILL HELP TO AVOID ANY LAST MINUTE DELAYS WITH YOUR CLOSING AND RECORDING.

END OF SCHEDULE B

（124ページから続く）

取特権などが記載されており、4項目にはローンの有無（この場合はない、ということ）が記載されています。

もうひとつ注目すべき点は、1ページ目の一番最後に、次の記述がしてあります。

AMERICAN LAND TITLE ASSOCIATION SHORT FORM RESIDENTIAL LOAN POLICY

ローンを組む場合、銀行は必ずこの「American Land Title」を要求します。これに対しローンがない場合、「California Land Title」になります。

この違いは、タイトル所有権チェックをカリフォルニア州にあるのか、アメリカ全体にするのか、という違いで、当然ながら銀行は、アメリカ全体の「American Land Title」を要求するということになります。

筆者のこの物件にはローンがないので、「California Land Title」とするところですが、最初に購入する際にローンを組んだため、「American Land Title」になっています。

これにより、物件のオーナーが誰で、ローンがある場合はローンの内容とか固定資産税が支払われているかどうかなどが、わかります。

このように**アメリカには日本の権利書と同様の書類はなく、当局で登録・記録されてい**

るかどうかが重要で、それをタイトル保険会社のレポートで確認することになります。

アメリカの不動産物件の所有権登録について、もう少し説明を加えておきます。アメリカは登録式で、上から順々に証書などの書類を重ねていきます。**(図表5-3)**

Aさん所有の物件をBさんに売却するとし、Bさんは購入に際してローンを組むとします。この売買が完了すると、Aさんは物件所有権をBさんに移転する・譲渡するという譲渡証書（Grant Deed）に署名します。また、Bさんはローンを組むので、銀行への抵当権設定証書（Deed of Trust）に署名します。銀行はこれで物件に抵当権を設定することになります。そうしますと、今までAさんの物件所有権証書の上にAさんの譲渡証書とローンの抵当権証書が登録され上乗せされます。

次にBさんがCさんに物件を売却するとします。Cさんはローンを組まず現金で買います。このときはBさんが譲渡証書に署名します。ここで重要なのは、Bさんのローン提供の銀行が抵当権設定証書を解除しなければなりませんが、銀行が「Reconveyance Deed」という証書を執行し、この証書を登録しないといけません。登録しないと、抵当権設定証書が残る形になってしまい、所有権がCさんだけではなくなる事態になります。実際にはそこはエスクローが「Reconveyance Deed」の確認と登録を手配し、タイトル保険会社が実際の登録をしますので、安心できます。

図表 5-3

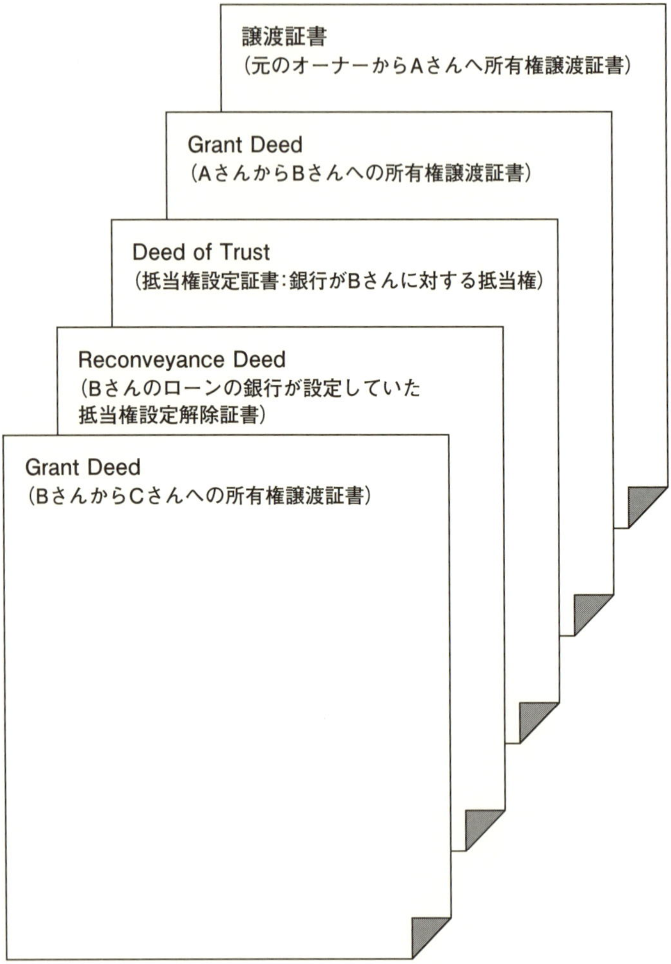

譲渡証書
（元のオーナーからAさんへ所有権譲渡証書）

Grant Deed
（AさんからBさんへの所有権譲渡証書）

Deed of Trust
（抵当権設定証書：銀行がBさんに対する抵当権）

Reconveyance Deed
（Bさんのローンの銀行が設定していた抵当権設定解除証書）

Grant Deed
（BさんからCさんへの所有権譲渡証書）

こぼれ話 5

ブームは終わりの始まり？

　一般に知れわたるようになり、多くの人たちが知るようになって参加しブームになれば、それはそのブームの終わりの始まりといえるでしょう。たとえばITバブル時の株式投資。家庭の主婦も株式投資をするまでブームになりましたが、結局短命でブームは去ってしまいました。例外はもちろんありますが、ほとんどの場合、世間に知れわたれば、もうその時点でピークは過ぎてしまっています。やはりきちんと勉強しいち早く先んずれば、必ずチャンスはつかめるし、お金持ちになれるのです。

　ある面白い記事がインターネットで出ていました。

　「金持ちになれる人はリスクよりもチャンスを見る。年収300万円の人はリスクを背負うことから逃げる。

　まず年収300万円の人は、何かあるとすぐにリスクを探し、リスクをみつけるのが非常にうまい。できない理由を探すのも天才的に上手です。そして、リスクがあるものはイヤだ、苦労するものはイヤだ、面倒くさいものはイヤだ……。そんな発想を持っています。チャンスがないという人は、無意識にそういう機会から逃げています。それがチャンスだとわかったときは、他の大あるいは周囲の人の様子を見ています。

勢の人も殺到しているから、もうチャンスではなくなっています。そして、『自分はチャンスに恵まれない』ということになるわけです。年収が1億円の人は、発想が逆で、まずリターンを見ます。リスクがあっても、それをひとつひとつ解決する方法を考える。あるいは乗り越える度胸がある。だからみんなが躊躇しているマーケットにいち早く飛び込める。投資では安いときに買えるし、ビジネスなら競合が少ないタイミングで参入できるから、大きく刈り取ることができるというわけです」

筆者がいつも提言しているのは、少数派にいることです。これはかなり勇気がいりますが、しっかりと勉強すれば、周りのことは気になりません。周りの人たちと同じことをすれば、同じ結果もしくはそれ以下の結果しか得られません。他人は関係ないのです。自分自身のことです。かの有名なウォーレン・バフェット氏が「投資のルールはシンプルで、他の人が欲張っているときには恐れを抱き、他の人が恐怖におののいている時に強欲になることだ」と言っています。要するに、少数派でいなさい、勇気をちなさい、ということです。

もちろん投資する際、怖いし失敗したらどうしようなど、ネガティブなことを考えがちですが、やはりしっかりと真剣に勉強することが肝要です。自分なりの信念やポリシーを持つことです。

第6章 改装(リフォーム)

1 レントコントロール

アメリカ不動産投資で利益率を上げるコツは、リフォーム改装を行って家賃を上げる方法があります。リフォームをするということは、テナントに退去してもらうわけですが、家賃値上げ通知をして退去してもらいます。通常10％以上の家賃値上げを行う場合、60日以上の事前通知が必要になりますが、10％以上50％や80％以上の値上げ通知を行いますので、たいていのテナントは退去します。ところがこの10％以上の値上げもできないところがあり、値上げ制限以外その他いろいろな条件や制約がある市もあって、まずこれら制約があろ市がどれなのかを知るところから始まります。この家賃値上げ制限等がある条例のことを「レントコントロール」といいます。

「レントコントロール」は、家賃の値上げに制限があり、家賃上昇が抑えられている制度です。テナントが継続的に住みたい場合、家賃の更新・値上げは通常年に1度で、値上げ幅は各市のレントコントロール条件によって異なります。ただし、テナントが退去した場

136

第6章
改装（リフォーム）

合は、新たに家賃が設定できますので、この限りではありません。また、この制限・条例はまずそれぞれの各市にあるかどうか、あった場合、制限はどれくらいか調べなければいけません。

たとえばロサンゼルス市のレントコントロールでは、年間の家賃値上げは、ここ最近年率3％になっています。基本的にインフレ率や費用の上昇に合わせているようです。また、1978年11月以降に建てられた物件は、レントコントロール対象外になります。

レントコントロールはサンタモニカ市が一番低く、年間1％程度で年によっては1％以下の時もあります。ときどき家賃が異常に低い部屋がありますが、何十年も前に入居したテナントです。たとえば20年前に入居したテナントの家賃が入居時1LDKで500ドルだったとします。現在の家賃相場は2500～3000ドルぐらいであるのに、その20年前に入居し続けている場合、家賃はせいぜい600ドル程度です。したがいまして、そういう方はなかなか退去しません。サンタモニカの物件で、よくとんでもなく低い家賃の部屋があったりしますので、購入しても利回りは極めて低くなります。リフォームをして家賃を上げようにも低いままですので、そうすることもできないのです。ただし、そういう状況でも退去してもらう方法はあります。

また、あまり知られていませんが、ビバリーヒルズ市もレントコントロールがあります。レントコントロールは家賃制限だけでなく、大家の責任なども規定しています。

もうひとつ、ニューポートビーチ、アーバイン、アナハイムなどのオレンジ郡は、現在レントコントロール規制がないのですが、制度化する動きがあって、2018年は議会で否決されましたが、近々規制される公算が強いとされています。

こういったレントコントロールがある市の物件を購入する場合、購入と同時に全員退去し、全室空室になるケースがありますので、そういう物件は絶好のチャンスです。

2 家賃相場

家賃相場が低いところは、いくらリフォームをしてもそれ相当の高い家賃にはなりません。実はこれも物件のロケーションにかかわってきます。やはり、ロケーションが良いところはリフォーム（改装）後の状態をテナントが理解し、それ相当の家賃を支払います。

ではどのようなところが好まれるのでしょうか。図表6-1に掲げる3つがあげられます。

よく言われるのが、「それだけの高額家賃を支払えるのだったら物件を買えばいいのに」と思うのですが、ほとんどの方がローンがおりないのです。まず頭金が十分にない。最低でも10％、普通は20％の頭金が必要です。

図表6-1の優良学校区、人気のエリアの物件は、2LDKで80万ドル以上します。そうであれば頭金は少なくとも8万ドル以上必要ですが、これだけのお金を貯金している人たちは少ないのが現状です。仮に両親から援助を受けても、ローン審査条件が厳しいので

図表6-1 ロケーションが良いところ

①学校区がよいところ
誰しも子どもは優良学校に通わせたいもの。しかしながら、優良学校区の物件は高額のため、かなりの高収入の家庭しか物件が購入できない。それでも良い学校に通わせたいのであれば、賃貸するしかないが、当然ながら家賃は高い部類に入る。

②限られたロケーション
ビーチの近くであったり、オーシャンヴューが全貌できるところなど、眺望が素晴らしいところや高級住宅街の一角など。

③人気のエリア
サンタモニカや世界一のヨットハーバーのマリナデルレイ、ビバリーヒルズは人気のエリアですが、当然物件価格や家賃が高いエリア。
最近の話題はシリコンバレーのIT企業群がその本部や第2本部をマリナデルレイを含めその近辺に引越ししている。そのため周りの住宅の価格やアパートの家賃の高騰が続いている。

10人に2～3人しか通りません。

厳しい条件の中で「2年以上の勤務年数」という条件がありますが、アメリカ人は少しでも良いポジションと給料の高いところにすぐに移りますので、転職したばかりという状態の人がほとんどです。高収入にもかかわらず、この条件を満たすことができなくてローンがおりないということが起こります。この融資条件は、政府系住宅ローン会社のFannie Mae、Freddie Macの条件で、各市中銀行はこれらの政府系保証を取り付けたいため、またローン債権を買い取ってもらうために、これらの政府系保証の条件を融資条件にします。

第6章
改装(リフォーム)

このような状況下、クレジット履歴が良く高収入の人たちでもローンが取れないことから、良いロケーションのところに住みたいため、高い家賃でも支払えるということになります。

前述のように、改装・リフォームの案件の必須条件は、次の3つです。

1 ロケーションが良いところ
2 メンテナンスが行き届いていない物件
3 周りの同様な物件の家賃が高く、家賃上昇のポテンシャルがある物件

これに信頼できる改装工事を受け持つリフォーム業者が、チームの一員に加わるかどうかが重要なポイントになります。この点は、地元の経験あるエージェントなどが十分にわかっています。

インターネットなどに出ている改装業者は、たいていゼネコン業者で、実際の工事は下請け業者に丸投げします。また、注文を取り付けたいため、見積り額を低く設定しますが、必ずといっていいほど、工事途中で値上げしてきます。当初の予定になかった事柄や、実際の工事が大変手間がかかることなどを理由に、かなり大幅に値上げしてきます。ある程

141

度は必要事項ですから致し方ないとしても、リフォームの仕上がりが一番大切です。良心的な改装業者をみつけることは、隠れた要因です。筆者も2〜3社の信頼できる実績ある業者をチームメンバーに入れて、改装リフォーム案件を何件も手がけています。

前述のような物件が見つかり、改装が仕上がりますと、家賃は当然ながらリフォーム前より高くなります。値上げ幅が大きくないと収益が多くならないので、売却価格が高くなりません。もうひとつのポイントは、この値上げ幅がどれくらいかということです。

後述しますアメリカ人パートナーの投資家グループは、16室のアパートを330万ドルで購入。うち198万ドルをローン。持ち出し金額は132万ドル。1LDKが8室で家賃が1100ドルから1350ドル、2LDKも8室で家賃が1500ドルから1750ドルでした。1年9か月ほどで14室も改装工事を終了し、1LDKの家賃は1850ドルから1950ドル、2LDKは2650ドルに上がりました。これを670万ドルで売却、改装工事代金を始め税金、エスクロー費用、タイトル費用、売買手数料などを差し引いても、おそらく250万ドルから270万ドルのネット利益を上げました。実際の使用持出し金額は132万ドルで、回収までの期間が1年9か月ですので、利回りは年率約50％ほどになります。

もう1件具体例をみてみましょう。**図表6-2**をご覧ください。

第6章
改装(リフォーム)

いくらリフォーム改装をしたからといって、49％〜114％アップの家賃が取れるのか、と疑問に思われるかもしれませんが、実はここがミソなのです。改装後の上質な状態の同じ部屋がいくらで貸し出しているかを、マーケット調査をして事前に知ることが必要になります。つまり、改装後の状態であればマーケット相場で高く貸せていれば問題ないわけです。周りに答えが出ているのです。

それから、改装期間ですが1LDK、2LDKともに3週間から1か月程度です。1部屋ずつ改装していきますと時間がかかりますので、2部屋を同時にやっていくような工程で4部屋ぐらいですと、合計2か月程度ぐらいで完成します。

また、この物件(案件番号<3))の長所は、1台分のガレージともう1台駐車できるパーキングスペースがあること。2LDKのひとつを除いて、3室全部にバスルームが2つ付いていることがあげられます。とくに駐車できる数が多いと人気が出ます。このレドンドビーチ、ハモサビーチ、マンハッタンビーチを始め、サンタモニカ、ブレントウッド、ベニス、マリナデルレイなど人気のエリアは駐車できるスペースの確保が極めて重要になります。

こういった細かな点も考慮し、改装リフォームをして収益を上げることを試算します。

(148ページに続く)

143

Cosmo Investment コスモ・インベストメント

v31

住所:2321 Pullman Lane, Redondo Beach, CA 90278

物件内容			運営支出 (売却$2.795M後推定)	
価格	$ 2,000,000	(売 2,795,000)	固定資産税(1.25%)	34,973
戸数	4		保険	1,800
建物面積(s.f., m2)	4,730	435m2	管理費($450/mo)	5,400
土地面積(s.f., m2)	7,494	689m2	AM費	
築年	1971		修理・維持費	1,000
建物比率	73%		電気	840
償却額 (4年)	2,040,350 円		ガス	0
CAP(推定ネット利回り) *	3.12%(1), 3.36%(2)		水道	4,800
年間償却額 ($1=110円) 1年	5,610万円		ゴミ	1,020
1戸当り価格	$ 500,000		ランドスケーピング	1,200
リノベーション費用:				
[内訳] 3Bed:11万円、2Bed:9万円	$ 200,000			
NOI (全改装後)	$ 87,443, 93,944		その他	1,000
取得費用 (推定)	約 30,000 円			
総コスト合計 * (推定)	$ 2,330,000 含販売手数料等		合計 (全改装後)	$ 52,033

収入			各戸内訳				
賃料	69240 141,600(1) 148,200(2)		戸数	タイプ	現賃料	改装後1	2
空室率(1.5%)	▲2,124 ▲2,223		2	3bd-2ba	平均1,612円	3,350円	3,500円
			1	2bd-2ba	1,550円	2,750円	2,850円
			1	2bd-1ba	995円	2,350円	2,500円
合計	69,240 139,476 145,977		4		5,770円	11,800円	12,350円

コメント	ロケーションはB+〜A-。賃貸契約は全室月決めのため、購入後2か月通知で賃料値上げ可能。但し3Bedの内1戸はエスクロー後空き。全改装後、売値279.5万ドルでCAP3.12%(1), CAP3.36%(2)となり、純利益46.5万円、見込む。

第6章
改装(リフォーム)

図表 6-2 具体例

購入価格	：200万ドル
現在の家賃	：3LDK（2室）平均1,612ドル
	2LDK（2室）それぞれ、995ドル、1,550ドル
購入時取得費用	：3万ドル

この条件でこの物件を購入したとします。

改装費用：
2LDKが45,000ドルで2室で90,000ドル
3LDKが55,000ドルで2室で11万ドル、合計20万ドル

改装後の家賃：
3LDKが3,350ドル～3,500ドル
2LDKが2,350ドル～2,850ドル

年間家賃：
141,600ドル～148,200ドル

現在の年間家賃：
69,240ドル約49％～114％の値上がり

経費：
（保守的に見積もって）年間52,033ドル

空室率1.5％を加味したNOI(Net Operating Income)：
87,443ドルから93,944ドル
希望売却価格279.5万ドルでCAP3.12％、3.36％

売却にかかる費用：
10万ドル
総コストは233万ドル（＝200万ドル購入価格＋購入費用3万ドル＋改装代20万ドル＋売却費用10万ドル）
279.5万ドルで売却できると、ネット利益は46.5万ドル見込める。
仮に30万ドルのネット利益の場合、売却価格は263万ドルになり、NOIは89,541ドルから96,042ドルになり、CAPは3.4％から3.65％に改善する。

第6章
改装(リフォーム)

(143ページから続く)

ターゲットとする利益が得られると試算し、確信できれば、物件購入に全力を尽くします。もちろん競争になれば価格を上げないと購入できませんので、いくらまで上げても大丈夫か、狙った利益は確保できるか、しっかりと試算しておかなければいけません。

筆者がロサンゼルスで親しくしているアメリカ人パートナーの投資家グループは、2004年からこのリフォーム・改装案件を50数件以上も手がけてきて、すべて成功しています。成功の秘けつは、やはり家賃が低いメンテナンスが行き届いていない物件をみつけることに尽きるそうです。彼らもいつも使っている改装業者がいて、彼らのチームに入れていますので、そういった物件をみつけさえすれば、リフォーム案件は成功したも同然になります。実は彼らが成功する秘けつが別にあって、改装仕上がった部屋の家賃が、相場よりも5%から10%高く貸せるようにしています。必ずしもすべての部屋に適用できるというわけではないのですが、筆者も同様に彼らのアイディアを共有しています。

次に具体的なリフォーム案件の実例を4つ紹介します。

最初の**実例1**は、関東の企業オーナーが、サンタモニカで7戸アパートを購入。サンタ

第6章 改装（リフォーム）

モニカはレントコントロールがあり、すぐにテナントを退去させることができないため、リフォーム改装案件には適していないのですが、売却と同時に退去するということで、すべて空室になるため購入後すぐに全室改装し、相場どおりの家賃でレントできることから、購入に踏み切りました。当然同じことを考えている投資家がいましたので、購入価格が上がりましたが、売主エージェントと誠実に交渉した結果、当方が買取契約を勝ち取りました。

7戸のうち1戸はレントコントロールで、低所得者向け用ということで家賃制限があったため、その部屋だけは必要最小限の改装に留め、その他全部の部屋を外装も含め全面改装しました。改装工事は、ビバリーヒルズからサンタモニカまで、建設や改装工事を手がけている地元の親子二代の業者に依頼しました。全面改装であったため、改装期間は5か月余りかかりましたが、家賃は2LDKで相場レベルの3000ドル前後に上げられました。購入金額は購入費用も含めて約310万ドル、改装工事代は約36万ドル、合計コストは約346万ドル。現在の市場相場売却予想価格は450万ドルと見込まれます。改装後のネット利回りCAPは約4.5％。

実例2は、東京の証券会社の部長様が優良学校区のランチョ・パロス・バーデス市のコ

（154ページへ続く）

実例1

befor

建物の横側

建物の横側

バスルーム

建物の後景

第6章
改装(リフォーム)

建物の前景

キッチン

建物の横側

after

建物の横側

キッチン

バスルーム

リビング

第6章
改装(リフォーム)

キッチン

エントランス

建物の前景

(149ページから続く)

ンドミニアムを55.5万ドルでご購入。ベランダからオーシャンビューの眺望があって高級感あり。もともと2LDKのコンドミニアムを前オーナーがまん中に仕切りの壁を取り付け、1LDKとワンルームの2戸にリノベーション。1LDKの家賃は1540ドル、ワンルームが1050ドルでしたが、改装して家賃はそれぞれ1950ドル、1350ドルに。27％以上の増収で、CAP利回りは4％近くに大幅に改善。改装費用は1万ドル強。

実例3は、東京の企業様が4戸のアパートをご購入。1部屋が4LDK、2部屋が2LDK、1部屋が1LDKで、購入（改装）前と購入（改装）後の家賃は、**図表6－3**に掲げました。本物件の2LDKの2部屋はバスルームが2つずつあるため、1つのバスルームの2LDKよりも高く貸せることが、本物件のポイントになります。同じ通りの2LDK（2バスルーム）の部屋は2750ドルで貸している実例があるため、2550ドルはまず確実といえます。改装後の物件価値は約40％上昇の見込みです。

実例4は、東京の会社部長職のお客様が55万ドルで優良学校区のタウンハウス（3ベッドルーム＋1バスルーム）をご購入。2台分のガレージ付きでパティオもあって人気が高いのですが、ベッドルームが3部屋あるにもかかわらず、バスルームがひとつということ

図表6-3 購入(改装)前と購入(改装)後の家賃

	1LDK	2LDK		4LDK
改装前	1,610ドル	1,780ドル	1,805ドル	3,250ドル
改装後	1,950ドル	2,550ドル	2,550ドル	4,000ドル

で、トイレだけの部屋にシャワーを新たに取り付け2バスルームに改装。同時にその他の部屋をきれいにグレードアップ。改装期間は約3週間、工事費は1・5万ドル弱。1バスルームだけであれば家賃は2500ドル前後のところ、シャワールームを追加したことで家賃は2800ドルへ上昇。

実例2

befor

バスルーム

バス・シャワールーム

キッチン

キッチン

第6章
改装(リフォーム)

after

ベッドルーム

シャワールーム

キッチン

キッチン

実例3

befor

キッチン

キッチン・リビング

バスルーム

バニティ

ベッドルーム

リビング

キッチン

キッチン

バスルーム

サンルーム

シャワールーム

第6章
改装（リフォーム）

工事中

リビング・キッチン

ユニットリビングダイニング

サンルーム

バスルーム

キッチン

ダイニングキッチン

キッチン

after

キッチン

バスルーム

キッチン

ダイニングキッチン

バスルーム

第6章
改装（リフォーム）

実例4

befor

建物前景

キッチン

バスルーム

リビング

after

キッチン

バスルーム

シャワールーム

リビングダイニング

トイレ

トイレ

こぼれ話 6

老後の資金

テレビ、新聞、雑誌、インターネットなどで、いまだに「老後資金はいくら必要か？」などと議論しています。これは全く無意味だということはおわかりですね。筆者が力説しているのは、いくらの資金が必要、いくら貯めるのではなく、いくらの収入をつくるか、なのです。

現役で生活しています現在、その生活費はどうやって賄っているでしょうか？貯金を切り崩して生活費に充てていますでしょうか？そうではなく、労働・仕事をして収入・給与を得て、その中から生活費を賄っています。退職し老後を過ごすということは、収入がなくなるということで、収入がなくなれば、たちどころに生活できなくなります。その収入の代わりに貯金をしておくということですが、仕事をして収入を得ている時と同じ状況であれば、生活はできるわけです。したがって現役時代にできるだけ早く収入が入る方法を考え、実行すればよいのです。

老後資金は、次の3つが主たる原資になりますが、これだけで安心できるでしょうか？

1　年金

2 貯金
3 個人年金（確定拠出型）

そもそも年金も本当にもらえるかどうかわからないですし、貯金も切り崩していくわけですから、どんどんなくなっていきます。なくなればなくなるほど、不安になっていきます。こんな老後は迎えたくないですね。では、どうすればよいのか？ 収入を生み出す資産を早く創り出すことです。この場合の収入・資産はできるだけ借金のないネットの収入・資産です。それではどうやってそれを創ればいいのでしょうか？

結論から言えば不動産投資です。「スタート資金がなくても投資はできます」と宣伝している不動産会社がありますが、やはり資金はある程度必要です。また、失敗しない不動産投資をするため、しっかりと勉強してもらいたいと思います。不動産投資関連の書籍は少なくとも5冊、できれば10冊以上読んでください。また、成功ばかりの本ではなく、失敗したとか損をしたという否定的な内容の書籍も大変参考になります。また、セミナーや勉強会にも参加、銀行の融資担当者とも仲良くなってください。

それから、得た情報は手帳かノートに書き込んでまとめることもお勧めします。これは思わね効力を発揮しますし、自分の財産になります。最短でも3か月、できれば6

か月から1年は勉強、実査してください。たとえば、あるマンションを購入し賃貸に回して家賃が毎月10万円とします。ここから、保険、税金などの諸経費およびローン支払い（ローンがあれば）を差し引いて手元に3万円残るとします。最初のうちは少額ですが、これが大きくまた戸数が増えれば、手取りネット収入は増えます。仮に同じような物件を10戸所有していますと、月のネット収入は30万円です。年収360万円になります。マンションではなくアパートを所有することも可能です。

このようにして、ネット収入を生み出す資産を所有することで、いつでもその収入が得られるのです。もちろん、物件の状態を常にチェックする必要はあり、場合によっては物件の入れ替えなどを行わなければなりません。よく家賃収入は「不労所得」といわれますが、とんでもないことです。物件を選択・購入し、テナントとの賃貸契約等々、手間暇かかるのです。テナント付け後も、修理など常に状態をチェックしておく必要があります。また「副業」などとも呼ばれますが、副業ではなく本業がもうひとつということで、自分自身の事業・ビジネスです。

第7章 売買取引と契約書

1 買付けオファーから合意に至るまで

アメリカの不動産売買契約書は、最初の買付けオファーの書類からスタートします。つまり、購入希望者が物件をいくらで、どんな条件で購入したいかなどを記入した買い付けオファーを売主に出状するところから開始します。

アメリカでは事前交渉はなく、この買い付けオファーを出すことによって、交渉がスタートするのです。購入したいと思えば、オファーを出すことによって手を上げないと、売主は誰が購入したいかわかりません。これぞと思った物件には、電光石火のごとく素早くオファーを出して、合意にこぎつけないといけません。こちらのオファーとの交渉が始まり合意に達するまでに他からのオファーが入れば、競争になります。そうしますと、価格も上がり売買条件も厳しくなります。ですから、気に入った物件があれば、間髪を入れずすぐにオファーを出し合意に至らないといけません。

お気づきかと思いますが、オファーを出し交渉して合意に至らないと、契約は成立しな

第7章
売買取引と契約書

いのです。多くの方がオファーを出す段階で契約すると勘違いします。オファーを出す＝契約完了ではないのです。オファー自体は何ら契約を拘束するものではありません。オファーでは、買手がいくらの価格で条件はこうで、と一方的に申し立てているに過ぎないのです。

また気に入った物件が数件ある場合は、全部の物件にオファーを出すほうが賢明なのです。筆者のお客様で以前3物件が気に入られ、第1希望の物件にオファーを入れたのですが、その際3物件同時にオファーを入れましょうとお勧めしたのですが、「3物件全部を購入するわけではない」と応じられませんでした。オファーを入れる段階で「購入することが決まったわけではない」と説明したのですが、ご理解には至りませんでした。結果第1物件は数回の交渉の結果、他者に取られ、次に2番目のご希望物件にオファーを入れてみると、これまた売買契約が成立していることが判明したため、それから第3希望の物件にオファーをすでに売買契約が成立していて、3物件とも購入するまでに至らなかったのです。もし最初に3物件同時にオファーを入れていれば、状況は全く変わっていたでしょう。

オファーを入れてそれから交渉し合意に至るまでの経緯を具体的に説明致します。今ある物件が50万ドルで売出されていたとし、買手の方がこれを50万ドル以下にできれば49万

ドル前後で購入したいとします。この時49万ドルでオファーを入れるより少し余裕を持って、たとえば48万ドルでオファーを出すことにします。また、この時点では他にまだオファーが入っていないとします。その他の条件として、30日間のエスクロー、デューデリジェンス（検査）期間21日間で、*エスクローはChicago Title Escrow、タイトル会社はChicago Title Company、現金買いのためローン条件はなしとします。これで作成したオファーが、**図表7－1**の買付け書類（オファー）です。

このオファーに対し、売手は価格は49・5万ドル、デューデリジェンス（検査）期間は10日間、エスクロー会社はFirst American Title Escrow、タイトル会社はFirst American Titleとカウンター（返答）してきました。このカウンターでエスクローの期間30日間は応諾しています（**図表7－2** Sellers' Counter Offer No.1）。

この時点で合意しなければいけない点は、次の4点です。

1　**価格**
2　エスクロー会社
3　タイトル会社
4　デューデリジェンス（検査）期間

第7章
売買取引と契約書

ここで検討するのは、合意に至るため先方の要望も受け入れるほうがよろしいので、こちらがより強く希望する点をカウンターし、その他は応じるとする方向で合意点を探ります。先方のエージェントとも十分に話し合い、合意するためにどこまで譲歩できるかを探ります。そこで「価格は49万ドル以下では売らない」、「エスクロー会社とタイトル会社はFirst American」でということになれば、デューデリジェンス（検査）期間は17日間にしてほしいことを条件に、こちら買手からのカウンターを作成します（**図表7-3** Buyer Counter No.1）。

これで売手が応諾したとしますと、やっと売買契約が合意に至ります。ここまでの書類、オファー、各カウンター書類すべてに売手、買手、それぞれのエージェントが署名し売買契約が成立します。

＊（注）エスクロー（escrow）とは、商取引の際に信頼の置ける第三者を仲介させて取引の安全を担保する第三者預託

不動産売買契約書（買付けオファー）

日付：[この日付は本契約書の作成日]

オファー：オファーする買手の名前。物件住所。オファー価格。エスクロー期間または締結日
[エスクロー期間とは、売買契約が合意してから最終売買完了日までの期間]

代理者（不動産エージェント）：売手と買手の代理者

融資条件：手付金額と3営業日以内の支払い
　全額現金買いかローン
　ローンの金額
　頭金と締結費用の資金証明
　鑑定評価が解除条件かどうか。
　条件解除の日数
　ローンが条件解除かどうか。
　条件解除の日数

第7章
売買取引と契約書

図表 7-1 買付け書類（オファー）

買手の物件売却：買手の物件売却が本契約の条件かどうか。

補足と助言：該当する各書類

その他条件：その他条件があれば、列記

費用の分担：
　物件実査、レポート、証明書など。
　法規制遵守項目
　エスクローとタイトル保険
　市や郡の譲渡税など。

第7章
売買取引と契約書

Property Address: *1234 Sample Street, Sample, CA 90000* Date: *April 1, 2018*

H. **VERIFICATION OF DOWN PAYMENT AND CLOSING COSTS:** Buyer (or Buyer's lender or loan broker pursuant to paragraph 3J(1)) shall, within 3 (or ___) **Days** After Acceptance, Deliver to Seller written verification of Buyer's down payment and closing costs. (☐ Verification attached.)

I. **APPRAISAL CONTINGENCY AND REMOVAL:** This Agreement is (or ☒ is NOT) contingent upon a written appraisal of the Property by a licensed or certified appraiser at no less than the purchase price. Buyer shall, as specified in paragraph 14B(3), in writing, remove the appraisal contingency or cancel this Agreement within 17 (or ___) **Days** After Acceptance.

J. **LOAN TERMS:**
(1) **LOAN APPLICATIONS:** Within 3 (or ___) **Days** After Acceptance, Buyer shall Deliver to Seller a letter from Buyer's lender or loan broker stating that, based on a review of Buyer's written application and credit report, Buyer is prequalified or preapproved for any NEW loan specified in paragraph 3D. If any loan specified in paragraph 3D is an adjustable rate loan, the prequalification or preapproval letter shall be based on the qualifying rate, not the initial loan rate. (☐ Letter attached.)
(2) **LOAN CONTINGENCY:** Buyer shall act diligently and in good faith to obtain the designated loan(s). Buyer's qualification for the loan(s) specified above **is a contingency** of this Agreement unless otherwise agreed in writing. If there is no appraisal contingency or the appraisal contingency has been waived or removed, then failure of the Property to appraise at the purchase price does not entitle Buyer to exercise the cancellation right pursuant to the loan contingency if Buyer is otherwise qualified for the specified loan. Buyer's contractual obligations regarding deposit, balance of down payment and closing costs **are not contingencies** of this Agreement.
(3) **LOAN CONTINGENCY REMOVAL:**
Within 21 (or ___) **Days** After Acceptance, Buyer shall, as specified in paragraph 14, in writing, remove the loan contingency or cancel this Agreement. If there is an appraisal contingency, removal of the loan contingency shall not be deemed removal of the appraisal contingency.
(4) ☐ **NO LOAN CONTINGENCY:** Obtaining any loan specified above is NOT a contingency of this Agreement. If Buyer does not obtain the loan and as a result does not purchase the Property, Seller may be entitled to Buyer's deposit or other legal remedies.
(5) **LENDER LIMITS ON BUYER CREDITS:** Any credit to Buyer, from any source, for closing or other costs that is agreed to by the Parties ("Contractual Credit") shall be disclosed to Buyer's lender. If the total credit allowed by Buyer's lender ("Lender Allowable Credit") is less than the Contractual Credit, then (i) the Contractual Credit shall be reduced to the Lender Allowable Credit, and (ii) in the absence of a separate written agreement between the Parties, there shall be no automatic adjustment to the purchase price to make up for the difference between the Contractual Credit and the Lender Allowable Credit.

K. **BUYER STATED FINANCING:** Seller is relying on Buyer's representation of the type of financing specified (including but not limited to, as applicable, all cash, amount of down payment, or contingent or non-contingent loan). Seller has agreed to a specific closing date, purchase price and to sell to Buyer in reliance on Buyer's covenant concerning financing. Buyer shall pursue the financing specified in this Agreement. Seller has no obligation to cooperate with Buyer's efforts to obtain any financing other than that specified in the Agreement and the availability of any such alternate financing does not excuse Buyer from the obligation to purchase the Property and close escrow as specified in this Agreement.

4. **SALE OF BUYER'S PROPERTY:**
A. This Agreement and Buyer's ability to obtain financing are NOT contingent upon the sale of any property owned by Buyer.
OR B. ☐ This Agreement and Buyer's ability to obtain financing are contingent upon the sale of property owned by Buyer as specified in the attached addendum (C.A.R. Form COP).

5. **ADDENDA AND ADVISORIES:**

A. ADDENDA:

Back Up Offer Addendum (C.A.R. Form BUO)	Addendum # ___ (C.A.R. Form ADM)
Septic, Well and Property Monument Addendum (C.A.R. Form SWPI)	Court Confirmation Addendum (C.A.R. Form CCA)
Short Sale Addendum (C.A.R. Form SSA)	Other

B. BUYER AND SELLER ADVISORIES:

Probate Advisory (C.A.R. Form PA)	☒ Buyer's Inspection Advisory (C.A.R. Form BIA)
Trust Advisory (C.A.R. Form TA)	Statewide Buyer and Seller Advisory (C.A.R. Form SBSA)
Short Sale Information and Advisory (C.A.R. Form SSIA)	REO Advisory (C.A.R. Form REO)
	Other

6. **OTHER TERMS:** *1. This is subject to inspection of the property.   2. Seller to provide Buyer with all the infromation of Section 14A within 5 days after Acceptance.   3. Seller to provide Buyer with all the keys including the garage openers of the seller's possession at close of escrow.*

7. **ALLOCATION OF COSTS**
A. **INSPECTIONS, REPORTS AND CERTIFICATES:** Unless otherwise agreed in writing, this paragraph only determines who is to pay for the inspection, test, certificate or service ("Report") mentioned; it **does not determine** who is to pay for any work recommended or identified in the Report.
(1) ☐ Buyer ☒ Seller shall pay for a natural hazard zone disclosure report, including tax ☒ environmental ☐ Other: ___
prepared by *Property ID*
(2) ☐ Buyer ☒ Seller shall pay for the following Report *Termite Inspection*
prepared by *(Seller's choice of any certified termite inspection company)*
(3) ☒ Buyer ☐ Seller shall pay for the following Report ___
prepared by *(Buyer's choice)*

Buyer's Initials (*T.N.*) (___)   Seller's Initials (___) (___)
RPA-CA REVISED 12/15 (PAGE 2 OF 10)
CALIFORNIA RESIDENTIAL PURCHASE AGREEMENT (RPA-CA PAGE 2 OF 10)

本売買契約に含まれるものと含まれないもの：たとえば冷蔵庫、洗濯機・乾燥機など、含まれるものと含まれないものを列記

第7章
売買取引と契約書

Property Address: *1234 Sample Street, Sample, CA 90000*   Date: *April 1, 2018*

B. GOVERNMENT REQUIREMENTS AND RETROFIT:
(1) ☐ Buyer ☒ Seller shall pay for smoke alarm and carbon monoxide device installation and water heater bracing, if required by Law. Prior to Close Of Escrow ("COE"), Seller shall provide Buyer written statement(s) of compliance in accordance with state and local Law, unless Seller is exempt.
(2) (i) ☐ Buyer ☒ Seller shall pay the cost of compliance with any other minimum mandatory government inspections and reports if required as a condition of closing escrow under any Law.
(ii) ☐ Buyer ☒ Seller shall pay the cost of compliance with any other minimum mandatory government retrofit standards required as a condition of closing escrow under any Law, whether the work is required to be completed before or after COE.
(iii) Buyer shall be provided, within the time specified in paragraph 14A, a copy of any required government conducted or point-of-sale inspection report prepared pursuant to this Agreement or in anticipation of this sale of the Property.

C. ESCROW AND TITLE:
(1) (a) ☒ Buyer ☒ Seller shall pay escrow fee *50 / 50 each own fees.*
  (b) Escrow Holder shall be *Chicago Title Escrow (Carolyn Gebhard)*
  (c) The Parties shall, within 5 (or ___) Days After receipt, sign and return Escrow Holder's general provisions.
(2) (a) ☐ Buyer ☒ Seller shall pay for **owner's** title insurance policy specified in paragraph 13E
  (b) Owner's title policy to be issued by *Chicago Title Company (Christine Gilmore)*
  (Buyer shall pay for any title insurance policy insuring Buyer's **lender**, unless otherwise agreed in writing.)

D. OTHER COSTS:
(1) ☐ Buyer ☒ Seller shall pay County transfer tax or fee
(2) ☐ Buyer ☒ Seller shall pay City transfer tax or fee
(3) ☐ Buyer ☒ Seller shall pay Homeowners' Association ("HOA") transfer fee
(4) Seller shall pay HOA fees for preparing documents required to be delivered by Civil Code §4525.
(5) ☐ Buyer ☒ Seller shall pay HOA fees for preparing all documents other than those required by Civil Code §4525.
(6) Buyer to pay for any HOA certification fee.
(7) ☐ Buyer ☒ Seller shall pay for any private transfer fee
(8) ☐ Buyer ☒ Seller shall pay for *Section 1 of Termite Report.*
(9) ☐ Buyer ☒ Seller shall pay for
(10) ☐ Buyer ☒ Seller shall pay for the cost, not to exceed $ *450.00* , of a standard (or ☒ upgraded) one-year home warranty plan, issued by *"Old Republic Home Protection* , with the following optional coverages: ☒ Air Conditioner ☐ Pool/Spa ☐ Other: *appliances, electricity, plumbing, etc.*
Buyer is informed that home warranty plans have many optional coverages in addition to those listed above. Buyer is advised to investigate these coverages to determine those that may be suitable for Buyer.
OR ☐ Buyer waives the purchase of a home warranty plan. Nothing in this paragraph precludes Buyer's purchasing a home warranty plan during the term of this Agreement.

8. ITEMS INCLUDED IN AND EXCLUDED FROM SALE:
A. **NOTE TO BUYER AND SELLER:** Items listed as included or excluded in the MLS, flyers or marketing materials are **not** included in the purchase price or excluded from the sale unless specified in paragraph 8 B or C.
B. **ITEMS INCLUDED IN SALE:** Except as otherwise specified or disclosed,
(1) All EXISTING fixtures and fittings that are attached to the Property;
(2) EXISTING electrical, mechanical, lighting, plumbing and heating fixtures, ceiling fans, fireplace inserts, gas logs and grates, solar power systems, built-in appliances, window and door screens, awnings, shutters, window coverings, attached floor coverings, television antennas, satellite dishes, air coolers/conditioners, pool/spa equipment, garage door openers/remote controls, mailbox, in-ground landscaping, trees/shrubs, water features and fountains, water softeners, water purifiers, security systems/alarms and the following if checked: ☐ all stove(s), except _____ ; ☐ all refrigerator(s) except _____ ; ☐ all washer(s) and dryer(s), except _____
(3) The following additional items:
(4) Existing integrated phone and home automation systems, including necessary components such as intranet and Internet-connected hardware or devices, control units (other than non-dedicated mobile devices, electronics and computers) and applicable software, permissions, passwords, codes and access information, are (☐ are NOT) included in the sale.
(5) **LEASED OR LIENED ITEMS AND SYSTEMS:** Seller shall, within the time specified in paragraph 14A, (i) disclose to Buyer if any item or system specified in paragraph 8B or otherwise included in the sale is leased, or not owned by Seller, or specifically subject to a lien or other encumbrance, and (ii) Deliver to Buyer all written materials (such as lease, warranty, etc.) concerning any such item. Buyer's ability to assume any such lease, or willingness to accept the Property subject to any such lien or encumbrance, is a contingency in favor of Buyer and Seller as specified in paragraph 14B and C.
(6) Seller represents that all items included in the purchase price, unless otherwise specified, (i) are owned by Seller and shall be transferred free and clear of liens and encumbrances, except the items and systems identified pursuant to 8B(5) and _____ , and (ii) are transferred without Seller warranty regardless of value.
C. **ITEMS EXCLUDED FROM SALE:** Unless otherwise specified, the following items are excluded from sale: (i) audio and video components (such as flat screen TVs, speakers and other items) if any such item is not itself attached to the Property, even if a bracket or other mechanism attached to the component or item is attached to the Property; (ii) furniture and other items secured to the Property for earthquake purposes; and (iii) _____ . Brackets attached to walls, floors or ceilings for any such component, furniture or item shall remain with the Property (or ☐ will be removed and holes or other damage shall be repaired, but not painted).

Buyer's Initials (*TN*) (_____)   Seller's Initials (_____) (_____)
RPA-CA REVISED 12/15 (PAGE 3 OF 10)
CALIFORNIA RESIDENTIAL PURCHASE AGREEMENT (RPA-CA PAGE 3 OF 10)

エスクロー締結と所有について：
物件所有はエスクロー締結日になるが、それ以外の場合の取決め

各法律条例と他の情報開示（鉛ペイント危険物情報公開含む）と契約解除権利

第7章
売買取引と契約書

Property Address: **1234 Sample Street, Sample, CA 90000** Date: **April 1, 2018**

9. CLOSING AND POSSESSION:
  A. Buyer intends (or ☐ does not intend) to occupy the Property as Buyer's primary residence
  B. **Seller-occupied or vacant property:** Possession shall be delivered to Buyer (i) at 6 PM or (☐ AM/ ☐ PM) on the date of Close Of Escrow; (ii) ☐ no later than ___ calendar days after Close Of Escrow; or (iii) ☐ at ___ ☐ AM/ ☐ PM on ___.
  C. **Seller remaining in possession After Close Of Escrow:** If Seller has the right to remain in possession after Close Of Escrow, (i) the Parties are advised to sign a separate occupancy agreement such as ☐ C.A.R. Form SIP, for Seller continued occupancy of less than 30 days, ☐ C.A.R. Form RLAS for Seller continued occupancy of 30 days or more, and (ii) the Parties are advised to consult with their insurance and legal advisors for information about liability and damage or injury to persons and personal and real property, and (iii) Buyer is advised to consult with Buyer's lender about the impact of Seller's occupancy on Buyer's loan.
  D. **Tenant-occupied property:** Property shall be vacant at least 5 (or ___) Days Prior to Close Of Escrow, unless otherwise agreed in writing. **Note to Seller: If you are unable to deliver Property vacant in accordance with rent control and other applicable Law, you may be in breach of this Agreement.**
  OR ☐ Tenant to remain in possession (C.A.R. Form TIP).
  E. At Close Of Escrow, Seller assigns to Buyer any assignable warranty rights for items included in the sale, and Seller shall Deliver to Buyer available Copies of any such warranties. Brokers cannot and will not determine the assignability of any warranties.
  F. At Close Of Escrow, unless otherwise agreed in writing, Seller shall provide keys, passwords, codes and/or means to operate all locks, mailboxes, security systems, alarms, home automation systems and intranet and Internet-connected devices included in the purchase price, and garage door openers. If the Property is a condominium or located in a common interest subdivision, Buyer may be required to pay a deposit to the Homeowners' Association ("HOA") to obtain keys to accessible HOA facilities.

10. STATUTORY AND OTHER DISCLOSURES (INCLUDING LEAD-BASED PAINT HAZARD DISCLOSURES) AND CANCELLATION RIGHTS:
  A. (1) Seller shall, within the time specified in paragraph 14A, Deliver to Buyer: (i) if required by Law, a fully completed: Federal Lead-Based Paint Disclosures (C.A.R. Form FLD) and pamphlet ("Lead Disclosures"); and (ii) unless exempt, fully completed disclosures or notices required by sections 1102 et. seq. and 1103 et. seq. of the Civil Code ("Statutory Disclosures"). Statutory Disclosures include, but are not limited to, a Real Estate Transfer Disclosure Statement ("TDS"), Natural Hazard Disclosure Statement ("NHD"), notice or actual knowledge of release of illegal controlled substance, notice of special tax and/or assessments (or, if allowed, substantially equivalent notice regarding the Mello-Roos Community Facilities Act of 1982 and Improvement Bond Act of 1915) and, if Seller has actual knowledge, of industrial use and military ordnance location (C.A.R. Form SPQ or ESD).
  (2) Any Statutory Disclosure required by this paragraph is considered fully completed if Seller has answered all questions and completed and signed the Seller section(s) and the Listing Agent, if any, has completed and signed the Listing Broker section(s), or, if applicable, an Agent Visual Inspection Disclosure (C.A.R. Form AVID). Nothing stated herein relieves a Buyer's Broker, if any, from the obligation to (i) conduct a reasonably competent and diligent visual inspection of the accessible areas of the Property and disclose, on Section IV of the TDS, or an AVID, material facts affecting the value or desirability of the Property that were or should have been revealed by such an inspection or (ii) complete any sections on all disclosures required to be completed by Buyer's Broker.
  Note to Buyer and Seller: Waiver of Statutory and Lead Disclosures is prohibited by Law.
  (4) Within the time specified in paragraph 14A, **(i)** Seller, unless exempt from the obligation to provide a TDS, shall, complete and provide Buyer with a Seller Property Questionnaire (C.A.R. Form SPQ); (ii) if Seller is not required to provide a TDS, Seller shall complete and provide Buyer with an Exempt Seller Disclosure (C.A.R. Form ESD).
  (5) Buyer shall, within the time specified in paragraph 14B(1), return Signed Copies of the Statutory, Lead and other disclosures to Seller.
  (6) In the event Seller or Listing Broker, prior to Close Of Escrow, becomes aware of adverse conditions materially affecting the Property, or any material inaccuracy in disclosures, information or representations previously provided to Buyer, Seller shall promptly provide a subsequent or amended disclosure or notice, in writing, covering those items. **However, a subsequent or amended disclosure shall not be required for conditions and material inaccuracies** of which Buyer is otherwise aware, or which **are disclosed in reports provided to or obtained by Buyer or ordered and paid for by Buyer.**
  (7) If any disclosure or notice specified in paragraph 10A(1), or subsequent or amended disclosure or notice is Delivered to Buyer after the offer is Signed, Buyer shall have the right to cancel this Agreement within **3 Days** After Delivery in person, or **5 Days** After Delivery by deposit in the mail, by giving written notice of cancellation to Seller or Seller's agent.
  B. **NATURAL AND ENVIRONMENTAL HAZARD DISCLOSURES AND OTHER BOOKLETS:** Within the time specified in paragraph 14A, Seller shall, if required by Law: **(i)** Deliver to Buyer earthquake guide(s) (and questionnaire), environmental hazards booklet, and home energy rating pamphlet; **(ii)** disclose if the Property is located in a Special Flood Hazard Area; Potential Flooding (Inundation) Area; Very High Fire Hazard Zone; State Fire Responsibility Area; Earthquake Fault Zone; and Seismic Hazard Zone; and **(iii)** disclose any other zone as required by Law and provide any other information required for those zones.
  C. **WITHHOLDING TAXES:** Within the time specified in paragraph 14A, to avoid required withholding, Seller shall Deliver to Buyer or qualified substitute, an affidavit sufficient to comply with federal (FIRPTA) and California withholding Law (C.A.R. Form AS or QS).
  D. **MEGAN'S LAW DATABASE DISCLOSURE:** Notice: Pursuant to Section 290.46 of the Penal Code, information about specified registered sex offenders is made available to the public via an Internet Web site maintained by the Department of Justice at **www.meganslaw.ca.gov.** Depending on an offender's criminal history, this information will include either the address at which the offender resides or the community of residence and ZIP Code in which he or she resides. (Neither Seller nor Brokers are required to check this website. If Buyer wants further information, Broker recommends that Buyer obtain information from this website during Buyer's inspection contingency period. Brokers do not have expertise in this area.)
  E. **NOTICE REGARDING GAS AND HAZARDOUS LIQUID TRANSMISSION PIPELINES:** This notice is being provided simply to inform you that information about the general location of gas and hazardous liquid transmission pipelines is available to the public via the National Pipeline Mapping System (NPMS) Internet Web site maintained by the United States Department of Transportation at **http://www.npms.phmsa.dot.gov/.** To seek further information about possible transmission pipelines near the Property, you may contact your local gas utility or other pipeline operators in the area. Contact information for pipeline operators is searchable by ZIP Code and county on the NPMS Internet Web site.
  F. **CONDOMINIUM/PLANNED DEVELOPMENT DISCLOSURES:**
  (1) SELLER HAS: 7 (or ___) Days After Acceptance to disclose to Buyer if the Property is a condominium, or is located in a planned development or other common interest subdivision (C.A.R. Form SPQ or ESD).

Buyer's Initials (TN) (_____)   Seller's Initials (_____) (_____)
RPA-CA REVISED 12/15 (PAGE 4 OF 10)
CALIFORNIA RESIDENTIAL PURCHASE AGREEMENT (RPA-CA PAGE 4 OF 10)

物件の状態

買手の物件調査と影響点

タイトル（所有権）と名義

Property Address: *1234 Sample Street, Sample, CA 90000* Date: *April 1, 2018*

(2) If the Property is a condominium or is located in a planned development or other common interest subdivision, Seller has 3 (or ___) Days After Acceptance to request from the HOA (C.A.R. Form HOA1): **(i)** Copies of any documents required by Law; **(ii)** disclosure of any pending or anticipated claim or litigation by or against the HOA; **(iii)** a statement containing the location and number of designated parking and storage spaces; **(iv)** Copies of the most recent 12 months of HOA minutes for regular and special meetings; and **(v)** the names and contact information of all HOAs governing the Property (collectively, "CI Disclosures"); **(vi)** private transfer fees; **(vii)** Pet fee restrictions; and **(viii)** smoking restrictions. Seller shall itemize and Deliver to Buyer all CI Disclosures received from the HOA and any CI Disclosures in Seller's possession. Buyer's approval of CI Disclosures is a contingency of this Agreement as specified in paragraph 14B(3). The Party specified in paragraph 7, as directed by escrow, shall deposit funds into escrow or direct to HOA or management company to pay for any of the above.

11. CONDITION OF PROPERTY: Unless otherwise agreed in writing: **(i)** the Property is sold **(a)** "AS-IS" in its PRESENT physical condition as of the date of Acceptance and **(b)** subject to Buyer's Investigation rights; **(ii)** the Property, including pool, spa, landscaping and grounds, is to be maintained in substantially the same condition as on the date of Acceptance; and **(iii)** all debris and personal property not included in the sale shall be removed by Close Of Escrow.
 A. Seller shall, within the time specified in paragraph 14A, DISCLOSE KNOWN MATERIAL FACTS AND DEFECTS affecting the Property, including known insurance claims within the past five years, and make any and all other disclosures required by law.
 B. Buyer has the right to conduct Buyer Investigations of the Property and, as specified in paragraph 14B, based upon information discovered in those investigations: (i) cancel this Agreement, or (ii) request that Seller make Repairs or take other action.
 C. Buyer is strongly advised to conduct investigations of the entire Property in order to determine its present condition. Seller may not be aware of all defects affecting the Property or other factors that Buyer considers important. Property Improvements may not be built according to code, in compliance with current Law, or have had permits issued.

12. BUYER'S INVESTIGATION OF PROPERTY AND MATTERS AFFECTING PROPERTY:
 A. Buyer's acceptance of the condition of, and any other matter affecting the Property, is a contingency of this Agreement as specified in this paragraph and paragraph 14B. Within the time specified in paragraph 14B(1), Buyer shall have the right, at Buyer's expense unless otherwise agreed, to conduct inspections, investigations, tests, surveys and other studies ("Buyer Investigations"), including, but not limited to: **(i)** a general physical inspection; **(ii)** an inspection specifically for wood destroying pests and organisms. Any inspection for wood destroying pests and organisms shall be prepared by a registered Structural Pest Control company; shall cover the main building and attached structures; may cover detached structures; shall NOT include water tests of shower pans on upper level units unless the owners of property below the shower consent; shall NOT include roof coverings; and, if the Property is a unit in a condominium or other common interest subdivision, the inspection shall include only the separate interest and any exclusive-use areas being transferred, and shall NOT include common areas; and shall include a report ("Pest Control Report") showing the findings of the company which shall be separated into sections for evident infestation or infections (Section 1) and for conditions likely to lead to infestation or infection (Section 2); **(iii)** inspect for lead-based paint and other lead-based paint hazards; **(iv)** satisfy Buyer as to any matter specified in the attached Buyer's Inspection Advisory (C.A.R. Form BIA); v) review the registered sex offender database; **(vi)** confirm the insurability of Buyer and the Property including the availability and cost of flood and fire insurance; and **(vii)** review and seek approval of leases that may need to be assumed by Buyer. Without Seller's prior written consent, Buyer shall neither make nor cause to be made: invasive or destructive Buyer Investigations, except for minimally invasive testing required to prepare a Pest Control Report; or inspections by any governmental building or zoning inspector or government employee, unless required by Law.
 B. Seller shall make the Property available for all Buyer Investigations. Buyer shall **(i)** as specified in paragraph 14B, complete Buyer Investigations and either remove the contingency or cancel this Agreement, and **(ii)** give Seller, at no cost, complete Copies of all such Investigation reports obtained by Buyer, which obligation shall survive the termination of this Agreement.
 C. Seller shall have water, gas, electricity and all operable pilot lights on for Buyer's Investigations and through the date possession is made available to Buyer.
 D. Buyer indemnity and seller protection for entry upon property: Buyer shall: **(i)** keep the Property free and clear of liens; **(ii)** repair all damage arising from Buyer Investigations; and **(iii)** indemnify and hold Seller harmless from all resulting liability, claims, demands, damages and costs. Buyer shall carry, or Buyer shall require anyone acting on Buyer's behalf to carry, policies of liability, workers' compensation and other applicable insurance, defending and protecting Seller from liability for any injuries to persons or property occurring during any Buyer Investigations or work done on the Property at Buyer's direction prior to Close Of Escrow. Seller is advised that certain protections may be afforded Seller by recording a "Notice of Non-Responsibility" (C.A.R. Form NNR) for Buyer Investigations and work done on the Property at Buyer's direction. Buyer's obligations under this paragraph shall survive the termination of this Agreement.

13. TITLE AND VESTING:
 A. Within the time specified in paragraph 14, Buyer shall be provided a current preliminary title report ("Preliminary Report"). The Preliminary Report is only an offer by the title insurer to issue a policy of title insurance and may not contain every item affecting title. Buyer's review of the Preliminary Report and any other matters which may affect title are a contingency of this Agreement as specified in paragraph 14B. The company providing the Preliminary Report shall, prior to issuing a Preliminary Report, conduct a search of the General Index for all Sellers except banks or other institutional lenders selling properties they acquired through foreclosure (REOs), corporations, and government entities. Seller shall within 7 Days After Acceptance, give Escrow Holder a completed Statement of Information.
 B. Title is taken in its present condition subject to all encumbrances, easements, covenants, conditions, restrictions, rights and other matters, whether of record or not, as of the date of Acceptance except for: **(i)** monetary liens of record (which Seller is obligated to pay off) unless Buyer is assuming those obligations or taking the Property subject to those obligations; and **(ii)** those matters which Seller has agreed to remove in writing.
 C. Within the time specified in paragraph 14A, Seller has a duty to disclose to Buyer all matters known to Seller affecting title, whether of record or not.
 D. At Close Of Escrow, Buyer shall receive a grant deed conveying title (or, for stock cooperative or long-term lease, an assignment of stock certificate or of Seller's leasehold interest), including oil, mineral and water rights if currently owned by Seller. Title shall vest as designated in Buyer's supplemental escrow instructions. THE MANNER OF TAKING TITLE MAY HAVE SIGNIFICANT LEGAL AND TAX CONSEQUENCES. CONSULT AN APPROPRIATE PROFESSIONAL.

Buyer's Initials (*TN*) (_____) Seller's Initials (_____) (_____)
RPA-CA REVISED 12/15 (PAGE 5 OF 10)
CALIFORNIA RESIDENTIAL PURCHASE AGREEMENT (RPA-CA PAGE 5 OF 10)

時間；条件解除；契約解除：
売主は7日間（または＿＿＿日間）以内に必要情報・書類を買手に渡す。
買手は物件実査、情報・書類、タイトル状況など17日間（または＿＿＿日間）以内に終了

第7章
売買取引と契約書

Property Address: **1234 Sample Street, Sample, CA 90000** Date: **April 1, 2018**

E. Buyer shall receive a CLTA/ALTA "Homeowner's Policy of Title Insurance", if applicable to the type of property and buyer. If not, Escrow Holder shall notify Buyer. A title company can provide information about the availability, coverage, and cost of other title policies and endorsements. If the Homeowner's Policy is not available, Buyer shall choose another policy, instruct Escrow Holder in writing and shall pay any increase in cost.

14. **TIME PERIODS; REMOVAL OF CONTINGENCIES; CANCELLATION RIGHTS: The following time periods may only be extended, altered, modified or changed by mutual written agreement. Any removal of contingencies or cancellation under this paragraph by either Buyer or Seller must be exercised in good faith and in writing (C.A.R. Form CR or CC).**

   A. **SELLER HAS: 7 (or 5) Days** After Acceptance to Deliver to Buyer all Reports, disclosures and information for which Seller is responsible under paragraphs 5, 6, 7, 8B(5), 10A, B, C, and F, 11A and 13A. If, by the time specified, Seller has not Delivered any such item, Buyer after first Delivering to Seller a Notice to Seller to Perform (C.A.R. Form NSP) may cancel this Agreement.

   B. (1) **BUYER HAS: 17 (or 21) Days** After Acceptance, unless otherwise agreed in writing, to: (i) complete all Buyer Investigations; review all disclosures, reports, lease documents to be assumed by Buyer pursuant to paragraph 8B(5), and other applicable information, which Buyer receives from Seller; and approve all matters affecting the Property; and (ii) Deliver to Seller Signed Copies of Statutory and Lead Disclosures and other disclosures Delivered by Seller in accordance with paragraph 10A.

   (2) Within the time specified in paragraph 14B(1), Buyer may request that Seller make repairs or take any other action regarding the Property (C.A.R. Form RR). Seller has no obligation to agree to or respond to (C.A.R. Form RRRR) Buyer's requests.

   (3) By the end of the time specified in paragraph 14B(1) (or as otherwise specified in this Agreement), Buyer shall Deliver to Seller a removal of the applicable contingency or cancellation (C.A.R. Form CR or CC) of this Agreement. However, if any report, disclosure or information for which Seller is responsible is not Delivered within the time specified in paragraph 14A, then Buyer has **5 (or ___) Days** After Delivery of any such items, or the time specified in paragraph 14B(1), whichever is later, to Deliver to Seller a removal of the applicable contingency or cancellation of this Agreement.

   (4) **Continuation of Contingency:** Even after the end of the time specified in paragraph 14B(1) and before Seller cancels, if at all, pursuant to paragraph 14D, Buyer retains the right, in writing, to either (i) remove remaining contingencies, or (ii) cancel this Agreement based on a remaining contingency. Once Buyer's written removal of all contingencies is Delivered to Seller, Seller may not cancel this Agreement pursuant to paragraph 14D(1).

   (5) Access to Property: Buyer shall have access to the Property to conduct inspections and investigations for **17 (or ___) Days** After Acceptance, whether or not any part of the Buyer's Investigation Contingency has been waived or removed.

   C. ☐ **REMOVAL OF CONTINGENCIES WITH OFFER: Buyer removes the contingencies specified in the attached Contingency Removal form (C.A.R. Form CR). If Buyer removes any contingency without an adequate understanding of the Property's condition or Buyer's ability to purchase, Buyer is acting against the advice of Broker.**

   D. **SELLER RIGHT TO CANCEL:**
   (1) **Seller right to Cancel; Buyer Contingencies:** If, by the time specified in this Agreement, Buyer does not Deliver to Seller a removal of the applicable contingency or cancellation of this Agreement, then Seller, after first Delivering to Buyer a Notice to Buyer to Perform (C.A.R. Form NBP), may cancel this Agreement. In such event, Seller shall authorize the return of Buyer's deposit, except for fees incurred by Buyer.

   (2) **Seller right to Cancel; Buyer Contract Obligations:** Seller, after first delivering to Buyer a NBP, may cancel this Agreement if, by the time specified in this Agreement, Buyer does not take the following action(s): (i) Deposit funds as required by paragraph 3A, or 3B or if the funds deposited pursuant to paragraph 3A or 3B are not good when deposited; (ii) Deliver a notice of FHA or VA costs or terms as required by paragraph 3D(3) (C.A.R. Form FVA); (iii) Deliver a letter as required by paragraph 3J(1); (iv) Deliver verification, or a satisfactory verification if Seller reasonably disapproves of the verification already provided, as required by paragraph 3C or 3H; (v) In writing assume or accept leases or liens specified in 8B5; (vi) Return Statutory and Lead Disclosures as required by paragraph 10A(5), or (vii) Sign or initial a separate liquidated damages form as required by paragraphs 3B and 21B, or (viii) Provide evidence of authority to sign in a representative capacity as specified in paragraph 19. In such event, Seller shall authorize the return of Buyer's deposit, except for fees incurred by Buyer.

   E. **NOTICE TO BUYER OR SELLER TO PERFORM:** The NBP or NSP shall: (i) be in writing; (ii) be signed by the applicable Buyer or Seller; and (iii) give the other Party at least **2 (or ___) Days** After Delivery (or until the time specified in the applicable paragraph, whichever occurs last) to take the applicable action. A NBP or NSP may not be Delivered any earlier than **2 Days** Prior to the expiration of the applicable time for the other Party to remove a contingency or cancel this Agreement or meet an obligation specified in paragraph 14.

   F. **EFFECT OF BUYER'S REMOVAL OF CONTINGENCIES:** If Buyer removes, in writing, any contingency or cancellation rights, unless otherwise specified in writing, Buyer shall conclusively be deemed to have: (i) completed all Buyer Investigations, and review of reports and other applicable information and disclosures pertaining to that contingency or cancellation right; (ii) elected to proceed with the transaction; and (iii) assumed all liability, responsibility and expense for Repairs or corrections pertaining to that contingency or cancellation right, or for the inability to obtain financing.

   G. **CLOSE OF ESCROW:** Before Buyer or Seller may cancel this Agreement for failure of the other Party to close escrow pursuant to this Agreement, Buyer or Seller must first Deliver to the other Party a demand to close escrow (C.A.R. Form DCE). The DCE shall: (i) be signed by the applicable Buyer or Seller; and (ii) give the other Party at least **3 (or ___) Days** After Delivery to close escrow. A DCE may not be Delivered any earlier than **3 Days** Prior to the scheduled close of escrow.

   H. **EFFECT OF CANCELLATION ON DEPOSITS:** If Buyer or Seller gives written notice of cancellation pursuant to rights duly exercised under the terms of this Agreement, the Parties agree to Sign mutual instructions to cancel the sale and escrow and release deposits, if any, to the party entitled to the funds, less fees and costs incurred by that party. Fees and costs may be payable to service providers and vendors for services and products provided during escrow. Except as specified below, **release of funds will require mutual Signed release instructions from the Parties, judicial decision or arbitration award.** If either Party fails to execute mutual instructions to cancel escrow, one Party may make a written demand to Escrow Holder for the deposit. (C.A.R. Form BDRD or SDRD). Escrow Holder, upon receipt, shall promptly deliver notice of the demand to the other Party. If, within 10 Days After Escrow Holder's notice, the other Party does not object to the demand, Escrow Holder shall disburse the deposit to the Party making the demand. If Escrow Holder complies with the preceding process, each Party shall be deemed to have released Escrow Holder from any and all claims or liability related to the disbursal of the deposit. Escrow Holder, at its discretion, may nonetheless require mutual cancellation instructions. **A Party may be subject to a civil penalty of up to $1,000 for refusal to sign cancellation instructions if no good faith dispute exists as to who is entitled to the deposited funds (Civil Code §1057.3).**

Buyer's Initials (_TN_) (_____)   Seller's Initials (_____) (_____)

RPA-CA REVISED 12/15 (PAGE 6 OF 10)

CALIFORNIA RESIDENTIAL PURCHASE AGREEMENT (RPA-CA PAGE 6 OF 10)

- 物件の最終確認:
買手はエスクロー締結の5日前に物件の最終確認・検証ができる。
- 修理:修理は買手の物件最終確認・検証の前に終了
- 固定資産税とその他の按分
- 不動産業者:報酬など。

- 代表・代理能力

- エスクローへの指示

第7章
売買取引と契約書

Property Address: **1234 Sample Street, Sample, CA 90000** Date: **April 1, 2018**

15. **FINAL VERIFICATION OF CONDITION:** Buyer shall have the right to make a final verification of the Property within **5 (or ___) Days** Prior to Close Of Escrow, NOT AS A CONTINGENCY OF THE SALE, but solely to confirm: **(i)** the Property is maintained pursuant to paragraph 11; **(ii)** Repairs have been completed as agreed; and **(iii)** Seller has complied with Seller's other obligations under this Agreement (C.A.R. Form VP).

16. **REPAIRS:** Repairs shall be completed prior to final verification of condition unless otherwise agreed in writing. Repairs to be performed at Seller's expense may be performed by Seller or through others, provided that the work complies with applicable Law, including governmental permit, inspection and approval requirements. Repairs shall be performed in a good, skillful manner with materials of quality and appearance comparable to existing materials. It is understood that exact restoration of appearance or cosmetic items following all Repairs may not be possible. Seller shall: **(i)** obtain invoices and paid receipts for Repairs performed by others; **(ii)** prepare a written statement indicating the Repairs performed by Seller and the date of such Repairs; and **(iii)** provide Copies of invoices and paid receipts and statements to Buyer prior to final verification of condition.

17. **PRORATIONS OF PROPERTY TAXES AND OTHER ITEMS:** Unless otherwise agreed in writing, the following items shall be PAID CURRENT and prorated between Buyer and Seller as of Close Of Escrow: real property taxes and assessments, interest, rents, HOA regular, special, and emergency dues and assessments imposed prior to Close Of Escrow, premiums on insurance assumed by Buyer, payments on bonds and assessments assumed by Buyer, and payments on Mello-Roos and other Special Assessment District bonds and assessments that are now a lien. The following items shall be assumed by Buyer WITHOUT CREDIT toward the purchase price: prorated payments on Mello-Roos and other Special Assessment District bonds and assessments and HOA special assessments that are now a lien but not yet due. Property will be reassessed upon change of ownership. Any supplemental tax bills shall be paid as follows: **(i)** for periods after Close Of Escrow, by Buyer, and **(ii)** for periods prior to Close Of Escrow, by Seller (see C.A.R. Form SPT or SBSA for further information). TAX BILLS ISSUED AFTER CLOSE OF ESCROW SHALL BE HANDLED DIRECTLY BETWEEN BUYER AND SELLER. Prorations shall be made based on a 30-day month.

18. **BROKERS:**
    A. **COMPENSATION:** Seller or Buyer, or both, as applicable, agree to pay compensation to Broker as specified in a separate written agreement between Broker and that Seller or Buyer. Compensation is payable upon Close Of Escrow, or if escrow does not close, as otherwise specified in the agreement between Broker and that Seller or Buyer.
    B. **SCOPE OF DUTY:** Buyer and Seller acknowledge and agree that Broker: **(i)** Does not decide what price Buyer should pay or Seller should accept; **(ii)** Does not guarantee the condition of the Property; **(iii)** Does not guarantee the performance, adequacy or completeness of inspections, services, products or repairs provided or made by Seller or others; **(iv)** Does not have an obligation to conduct an inspection of common areas or areas off the site of the Property; **(v)** Shall not be responsible for identifying defects on the Property, in common areas, or offsite unless such defects are visually observable by an inspection of reasonably accessible areas of the Property or are known to Broker; **(vi)** Shall not be responsible for inspecting public records or permits concerning the title or use of Property; **(vii)** Shall not be responsible for identifying the location of boundary lines or other items affecting title; **(viii)** Shall not be responsible for verifying square footage, representations of others or information contained in Investigation reports, Multiple Listing Service, advertisements, flyers or other promotional material; **(ix)** Shall not be responsible for determining the fair market value of the Property or any personal property included in the sale; **(x)** Shall not be responsible for providing legal or tax advice regarding any aspect of a transaction entered into by Buyer or Seller; and **(xi)** Shall not be responsible for providing other advice or information that exceeds the knowledge, education and experience required to perform real estate licensed activity. Buyer and Seller agree to seek legal, tax, insurance, title and other desired assistance from appropriate professionals.

19. **REPRESENTATIVE CAPACITY:** If one or more Parties is signing this Agreement in a representative capacity and not for him/herself as an individual then that Party shall so indicate in paragraph 31 or 32 and attach a Representative Capacity Signature Disclosure (C.A.R. Form RCSD). Wherever the signature or initials of the representative identified in the RCSD appear on this Agreement or any related documents, it shall be deemed to be in a representative capacity for the entity described and not in an individual capacity, unless otherwise indicated. The Party acting in a representative capacity (i) represents that the entity for which that party is acting already exists and (ii) shall Deliver to the other Party and Escrow Holder, within **3 Days** After Acceptance, evidence of authority to act in that capacity (such as but not limited to: applicable portion of the trust or Certification Of Trust (Probate Code §18100.5), letters testamentary, court order, power of attorney, corporate resolution, or formation documents of the business entity).

20. **JOINT ESCROW INSTRUCTIONS TO ESCROW HOLDER:**
    A. The following paragraphs, or applicable portions thereof, of this Agreement constitute the joint escrow instructions **of Buyer and Seller to Escrow Holder,** which Escrow Holder is to use along with any related counter offers and addenda, and any additional mutual instructions to close the escrow: paragraphs 1, 3, 4B, 5A, 6, 7, 10C, 13, 14H, 17, 18A, 19, 20, 26, 29, 30, 31, 32 and paragraph D of the section titled Real Estate Brokers on page 10. If a Copy of the separate compensation agreement(s) provided for in paragraph 18A, or paragraph D of the section titled Real Estate Brokers on page 10 is deposited with Escrow Holder by Broker, Escrow Holder shall accept such agreement(s) and pay out from Buyer's or Seller's funds, or both, as applicable, the Broker's compensation provided for in such agreement(s). The terms and conditions of this Agreement not set forth in the specified paragraphs are additional matters for the information of Escrow Holder, but about which Escrow Holder need not be concerned. Buyer and Seller will receive Escrow Holder's general provisions, if any, directly from Escrow Holder and will execute such provisions within the time specified in paragraph 7C(1)(c). To the extent the general provisions are inconsistent or conflict with this Agreement, the general provisions will control as to the duties and obligations of Escrow Holder only. Buyer and Seller will execute additional instructions, documents and forms provided by Escrow Holder that are reasonably necessary to close the escrow and, as directed by Escrow Holder, within **3 (or ___) Days,** shall pay to Escrow Holder or HOA or HOA management company or others any fee required by paragraphs 7, 10 or elsewhere in this Agreement.
    B. A Copy of this Agreement including any counter offer(s) and addenda shall be delivered to Escrow Holder within **3 Days** After Acceptance (or ___). Buyer and Seller authorize Escrow Holder to accept and rely on Copies and Signatures as defined in this Agreement as originals, to open escrow and for other purposes of escrow. The validity of this Agreement as between Buyer and Seller is not affected by whether or when Escrow Holder Signs this Agreement. Escrow Holder shall provide Seller's Statement of Information to Title company when received from Seller. If Seller delivers an affidavit to Escrow Holder to satisfy Seller's FIRPTA obligation under paragraph 10C, Escrow Holder shall deliver to Buyer a Qualified Substitute statement that complies with federal Law.

Buyer's Initials (**IN**) (___) Seller's Initials (___) (___)
RPA-CA REVISED 12/15 (PAGE 7 OF 10)
CALIFORNIA RESIDENTIAL PURCHASE AGREEMENT (RPA-CA PAGE 7 OF 10)

買手の契約不履行の救済

論争解決：調停による解決

第7章
売買取引と契約書

Property Address: *1234 Sample Street, Sample, CA 90000* Date: *April 1, 2018*

C. Brokers are a party to the escrow for the sole purpose of compensation pursuant to paragraph 18A and paragraph D of the section titled Real Estate Brokers on page 10. Buyer and Seller irrevocably assign to Brokers compensation specified in paragraph 18A, and irrevocably instruct Escrow Holder to disburse those funds to Brokers at Close Of Escrow or pursuant to any other mutually executed cancellation agreement. Compensation instructions can be amended or revoked only with the written consent of Brokers. Buyer and Seller shall release and hold harmless Escrow Holder from any liability resulting from Escrow Holder's payment to Broker(s) of compensation pursuant to this Agreement.

D. Upon receipt, Escrow Holder shall provide Seller and Seller's Broker verification of Buyer's deposit of funds pursuant to paragraph 3A and 3B. Once Escrow Holder becomes aware of any of the following, Escrow Holder shall immediately notify all Brokers: (i) if Buyer's initial or any additional deposit or down payment is not made pursuant to this Agreement, or is not good at time of deposit with Escrow Holder; or (ii) if Buyer and Seller instruct Escrow Holder to cancel escrow.

E. A Copy of any amendment that affects any paragraph of this Agreement for which Escrow Holder is responsible shall be delivered to Escrow Holder within 3 Days after mutual execution of the amendment.

21. REMEDIES FOR BUYER'S BREACH OF CONTRACT: ←

A. Any clause added by the Parties specifying a remedy (such as release or forfeiture of deposit or making a deposit non-refundable) for failure of Buyer to complete the purchase in violation of this Agreement shall be deemed invalid unless the clause independently satisfies the statutory liquidated damages requirements set forth in the Civil Code.

B. **LIQUIDATED DAMAGES:** If Buyer fails to complete this purchase because of Buyer's default, Seller shall retain, as liquidated damages, the deposit actually paid. If the Property is a dwelling with no more than four units, one of which Buyer intends to occupy, then the amount retained shall be no more than 3% of the purchase price. Any excess shall be returned to Buyer. Except as provided in paragraph 14H, release of funds will require mutual, Signed release instructions from both Buyer and Seller, judicial decision or arbitration award. **AT THE TIME OF ANY INCREASED DEPOSIT BUYER AND SELLER SHALL SIGN A SEPARATE LIQUIDATED DAMAGES PROVISION INCORPORATING THE INCREASED DEPOSIT AS LIQUIDATED DAMAGES (C.A.R. FORM RID).**

Buyer's Initials *TN* / ____ Seller's Initials ____ / ____

22. DISPUTE RESOLUTION: ←

A. **MEDIATION:** The Parties agree to mediate any dispute or claim arising between them out of this Agreement, or any resulting transaction, before resorting to arbitration or court action through the C.A.R. Real Estate Mediation Center for Consumers (www.consumermediation.org) or through any other mediation provider or service mutually agreed to by the Parties. The Parties also agree to mediate any disputes or claims with Broker(s), who, in writing, agree to such mediation prior to, or within a reasonable time after, the dispute or claim is presented to the Broker. Mediation fees, if any, shall be divided equally among the Parties involved. If, for any dispute or claim to which this paragraph applies, any Party (i) commences an action without first attempting to resolve the matter through mediation, or (ii) before commencement of an action, refuses to mediate after a request has been made, then that Party shall not be entitled to recover attorney fees, even if they would otherwise be available to that Party in any such action. THIS MEDIATION PROVISION APPLIES WHETHER OR NOT THE ARBITRATION PROVISION IS INITIALED. Exclusions from this mediation agreement are specified in paragraph 22C.

B. **ARBITRATION OF DISPUTES:**
The Parties agree that any dispute or claim in Law or equity arising between them out of this Agreement or any resulting transaction, which is not settled through mediation, shall be decided by neutral, binding arbitration. The Parties also agree to arbitrate any disputes or claims with Broker(s), who, in writing, agree to such arbitration prior to, or within a reasonable time after, the dispute or claim is presented to the Broker. The arbitrator shall be a retired judge or justice, or an attorney with at least 5 years of residential real estate Law experience, unless the parties mutually agree to a different arbitrator. The Parties shall have the right to discovery in accordance with Code of Civil Procedure §1283.05. In all other respects, the arbitration shall be conducted in accordance with Title 9 of Part 3 of the Code of Civil Procedure. Judgment upon the award of the arbitrator(s) may be entered into any court having jurisdiction. Enforcement of this agreement to arbitrate shall be governed by the Federal Arbitration Act. Exclusions from this arbitration agreement are specified in paragraph 22C.

"NOTICE: BY INITIALING IN THE SPACE BELOW YOU ARE AGREEING TO HAVE ANY DISPUTE ARISING OUT OF THE MATTERS INCLUDED IN THE 'ARBITRATION OF DISPUTES' PROVISION DECIDED BY NEUTRAL ARBITRATION AS PROVIDED BY CALIFORNIA LAW AND YOU ARE GIVING UP ANY RIGHTS YOU MIGHT POSSESS TO HAVE THE DISPUTE LITIGATED IN A COURT OR JURY TRIAL. BY INITIALING IN THE SPACE BELOW YOU ARE GIVING UP YOUR JUDICIAL RIGHTS TO DISCOVERY AND APPEAL, UNLESS THOSE RIGHTS ARE SPECIFICALLY INCLUDED IN THE 'ARBITRATION OF DISPUTES' PROVISION. IF YOU REFUSE TO SUBMIT TO ARBITRATION AFTER AGREEING TO THIS PROVISION, YOU MAY BE COMPELLED TO ARBITRATE UNDER THE AUTHORITY OF THE CALIFORNIA CODE OF CIVIL PROCEDURE. YOUR AGREEMENT TO THIS ARBITRATION PROVISION IS VOLUNTARY."

"WE HAVE READ AND UNDERSTAND THE FOREGOING AND AGREE TO SUBMIT DISPUTES ARISING OUT OF THE MATTERS INCLUDED IN THE 'ARBITRATION OF DISPUTES' PROVISION TO NEUTRAL ARBITRATION."

Buyer's Initials *TN* / ____ Seller's Initials ____ / ____

C. **ADDITIONAL MEDIATION AND ARBITRATION TERMS:**
(1) **EXCLUSIONS:** The following matters are excluded from mediation and arbitration: (i) a judicial or non-judicial foreclosure or other action or proceeding to enforce a deed of trust, mortgage or installment land sale contract as defined in Civil Code §2985; (ii) an unlawful detainer action; and (iii) any matter that is within the jurisdiction of a probate, small claims or bankruptcy court.

Buyer's Initials (*TN*) (____) Seller's Initials (____) (____)

RPA-CA REVISED 12/15 (PAGE 8 OF 10)

CALIFORNIA RESIDENTIAL PURCHASE AGREEMENT (RPA-CA PAGE 8 OF 10)

- 販売・サービス業者の選定
- MLS（Multiple Listing Service）：
  不動産業者間の物件情報掲載サービス
- 弁護士費用：
  論争の場合、勝訴側が弁護士費用を受諾できる。
- 譲渡：買手は売手の書面による承諾なしで本契約の権利を譲渡できない。
- 公平・平等住居機会：
  連邦、州および地元の反差別法律に従う。
- オファーの条件
- 時間；契約全体；変更
- 定義：本契約中の文言の定義
- オファーの失効期限：
  下記買手の署名日付の3日後の午後5時に本オファーは失効
  日付＿＿＿＿＿＿＿＿＿＿
  買手署名＿＿＿＿＿＿＿＿＿＿＿＿＿＿＿＿＿＿＿＿

第7章
売買取引と契約書

Property Address: 1234 Sample Street, Sample, CA 90000 Date: **April 1, 2018**

(2) **PRESERVATION OF ACTIONS:** The following shall not constitute a waiver nor violation of the mediation and arbitration provisions: (i) the filing of a court action to preserve a statute of limitations; (ii) the filing of a court action to enable the recording of a notice of pending action, for order of attachment, receivership, injunction, or other provisional remedies; or (iii) the filing of a mechanic's lien.

(3) **BROKERS:** Brokers shall not be obligated nor compelled to mediate or arbitrate unless they agree to do so in writing. Any Broker(s) participating in mediation or arbitration shall not be deemed a party to this Agreement.

23. **SELECTION OF SERVICE PROVIDERS:** Brokers do not guarantee the performance of any vendors, service or product providers ("Providers"), whether referred by Broker or selected by Buyer, Seller or other person. Buyer and Seller may select ANY Providers of their own choosing.

24. **MULTIPLE LISTING SERVICE ("MLS")** Brokers are authorized to report to the MLS a pending sale and, upon Close Of Escrow, the sales price and other terms of this transaction shall be provided to the MLS to be published and disseminated to persons and entities authorized to use the information on terms approved by the MLS.

25. **ATTORNEY FEES:** In any action, proceeding, or arbitration between Buyer and Seller arising out of this Agreement, the prevailing Buyer or Seller shall be entitled to reasonable attorney fees and costs from the non-prevailing Buyer or Seller, except as provided in paragraph 22A.

26. **ASSIGNMENT:** Buyer shall not assign all or any part of Buyer's interest in this Agreement without first having obtained the separate written consent of Seller to a specified assignee. Such consent shall not be unreasonably withheld. Any total or partial assignment shall not relieve Buyer of Buyer's obligations pursuant to this Agreement unless otherwise agreed in writing by Seller. (C.A.R. Form AOAA).

27. **EQUAL HOUSING OPPORTUNITY:** The Property is sold in compliance with federal, state and local anti-discrimination Laws.

28. **TERMS AND CONDITIONS OF OFFER:**
This is an offer to purchase the Property on the above terms and conditions. The liquidated damages paragraph or the arbitration of disputes paragraph is incorporated in this Agreement if initialed by all Parties or if incorporated by mutual agreement in a counter offer or addendum. If at least one but not all Parties initial, a counter offer is required until agreement is reached. Seller has the right to continue to offer the Property for sale and to accept any other offer at any time prior to notification of Acceptance. The Parties have read and acknowledge receipt of a Copy of the offer and agree to the confirmation of agency relationships. If this offer is accepted and Buyer subsequently defaults, Buyer may be responsible for payment of Brokers' compensation. This Agreement and any supplement, addendum or modification, including any Copy, may be Signed in two or more counterparts, all of which shall constitute one and the same writing.

29. **TIME OF ESSENCE; ENTIRE CONTRACT; CHANGES:** Time is of the essence. All understandings between the Parties are incorporated in this Agreement. Its terms are intended by the Parties as a final, complete and exclusive expression of their Agreement with respect to its subject matter, and may not be contradicted by evidence of any prior agreement or contemporaneous oral agreement. If any provision of this Agreement is held to be ineffective or invalid, the remaining provisions will nevertheless be given full force and effect. Except as otherwise specified, this Agreement shall be interpreted and disputes shall be resolved in accordance with the Laws of the State of California. **Neither this Agreement nor any provision in it may be extended, amended, modified, altered or changed, except in writing Signed by Buyer and Seller.**

30. **DEFINITIONS:** As used in this Agreement:
   A. **"Acceptance"** means the time the offer or final counter offer is accepted in writing by a Party and is delivered to and personally received by the other Party or that Party's authorized agent in accordance with the terms of this offer or a final counter offer.
   B. **"Agreement"** means this document and any counter offers and any incorporated addenda, collectively forming the binding agreement between the Parties. Addenda are incorporated only when Signed by all Parties.
   C. **"C.A.R. Form"** means the most current version of the specific form referenced or another comparable form agreed to by the parties.
   D. **"Close Of Escrow"**, including "COE", means the date the grant deed, or other evidence of transfer of title, is recorded.
   E. **"Copy"** means copy by any means including photocopy, NCR, facsimile and electronic.
   F. **"Days"** means calendar days. However, after Acceptance, the last **Day** for performance of any act required by this Agreement (including Close Of Escrow) shall not include any Saturday, Sunday, or legal holiday and shall instead be the next Day.
   G. **"Days After"** means the specified number of calendar days after the occurrence of the event specified, not counting the calendar date on which the specified event occurs, and ending at 11:59 PM on the final day.
   H. **"Days Prior"** means the specified number of calendar days before the occurrence of the event specified, not counting the calendar date on which the specified event is scheduled to occur.
   I. **"Deliver", "Delivered"** or **"Delivery"**, unless otherwise specified in writing, means and shall be effective upon: personal receipt by Buyer or Seller or the individual Real Estate Licensee for that principal as specified in the section titled Real Estate Brokers on page 10, regardless of the method used (i.e., messenger, mail, email, fax, other).
   J. **"Electronic Copy"** or **"Electronic Signature"** means, as applicable, an electronic copy or signature complying with California Law. Buyer and Seller agree that electronic means will not be used by either party to modify or alter the content or integrity of this Agreement without the knowledge and consent of the other Party.
   K. **"Law"** means any law, code, statute, ordinance, regulation, rule or order, which is adopted by a controlling city, county, state or federal legislative, judicial or executive body or agency.
   L. **"Repairs"** means any repairs (including pest control), alterations, replacements, modifications or retrofitting of the Property provided for under this Agreement.
   M. **"Signed"** means either a handwritten or electronic signature on an original document, Copy or any counterpart.

31. **EXPIRATION OF OFFER:** This offer shall be deemed revoked and the deposit, if any, shall be returned to Buyer unless the offer is Signed by Seller and a Copy of the Signed offer is personally received by Buyer, or by _____ who is authorized to receive it, by 5:00 PM on the third Day after this offer is signed by Buyer (or by ☐ _____ ☐ AM/ ☐ PM, on _____ (date)).

☐ One or more Buyers is signing this Agreement in a representative capacity and not for him/herself as an individual. See attached Representative Capacity Signature Disclosure (C.A.R. Form RCSD-B) for additional terms.

Date **04/01/2018** BUYER *Taro Nippon*
(Print name) **Taro Nippon**
Date _____ BUYER _____
(Print name) _____

☐ Additional Signature Addendum attached (C.A.R. Form ASA).

Seller's Initials (_____) (_____)

RPA-CA REVISED 12/15 (PAGE 9 OF 10)
CALIFORNIA RESIDENTIAL PURCHASE AGREEMENT (RPA-CA PAGE 9 OF 10)

オファーの応諾：
売手は本契約のオファーを受諾する。(ただし、売手のカウンター・オファーを添付)
日付_____
売手署名_____

第7章
売買取引と契約書

Property Address: *1234 Sample Street, Sample, CA 90000*   Date: *April 1, 2018*

32. ACCEPTANCE OF OFFER: Seller warrants that Seller is the owner of the Property, or has the authority to execute this Agreement. Seller accepts the above offer, and agrees to sell the Property on the above terms and conditions. Seller has read and acknowledges receipt of a Copy of this Agreement, and authorizes Broker to Deliver a Signed Copy to Buyer.

☐ (If checked) **SELLER'S ACCEPTANCE IS SUBJECT TO ATTACHED COUNTER OFFER (C.A.R. Form SCO or SMCO) DATED:**

☐ One or more Sellers is signing this Agreement in a representative capacity and not for him/herself as an individual. See attached Representative Capacity Signature Disclosure (C.A.R. Form RCSD-S) for additional terms.

Date _____ SELLER _____
(Print name)
Date _____ SELLER _____
(Print name)

☐ Additional Signature Addendum attached (C.A.R. Form ASA).

(___ / ___) (Do not initial if making a counter offer.) **CONFIRMATION OF ACCEPTANCE:** A Copy of Signed Acceptance was
(Initials) personally received by Buyer or Buyer's authorized agent on (date) _____ at _____ AM / PM. A binding Agreement is created when a Copy of Signed Acceptance is personally received by Buyer or Buyer's authorized agent whether or not confirmed in this document. Completion of this confirmation is not legally required in order to create a binding Agreement; it is solely intended to evidence the date that **Confirmation of Acceptance has occurred.**

REAL ESTATE BROKERS:
A. Real Estate Brokers are not parties to the Agreement between Buyer and Seller.
B. Agency relationships are confirmed as stated in paragraph 2.
C. If specified in paragraph 3A(2), Agent who submitted the offer for Buyer acknowledges receipt of deposit.
D. **COOPERATING BROKER COMPENSATION:** Listing Broker agrees to pay Cooperating Broker (**Selling Firm**) and Cooperating Broker agrees to accept, out of Listing Broker's proceeds in escrow, the amount specified in the MLS, provided Cooperating Broker is a Participant of the MLS in which the Property is offered for sale or a reciprocal MLS. If Listing Broker and Cooperating Broker are not both Participants of the MLS, or a reciprocal MLS, in which the Property is offered for sale, then compensation must be specified in a separate written agreement (C.A.R. Form CBC). Declaration of License and Tax (C.A.R. Form DLT) may be used to document that tax reporting will be required or that an exemption exists.

Real Estate Broker (Selling Firm) *Cosmo Investment*   CalBRE Lic. *# 01111885*
By *Norio Kanai*   *Norio Kanai* CalBRE Lic. *# 01111885*   Date *04/01/2018*
By _____ CalBRE Lic. # _____ Date _____
Address *2512 Artesia Blvd., Suite 250-D*   City *Redondo Beach*   State *CA*   Zip *90278*
Telephone *(310)782-4657*   Fax _____ E-mail *cosmokanai@gmail.com*
Real Estate Broker (Listing Firm) *Seller's Realty*   CalBRE Lic. #
By _____ CalBRE Lic. # _____ Date _____
By _____ CalBRE Lic. # _____ Date _____
Address _____ City _____ State *CA*   Zip _____
Telephone _____ Fax _____ E-mail _____

ESCROW HOLDER ACKNOWLEDGMENT:
Escrow Holder acknowledges receipt of a Copy of this Agreement, (if checked, ☐ a deposit in the amount of $ _____),
counter offer numbers _____ ☐ Seller's Statement of Information and _____, and agrees to act as Escrow Holder subject to paragraph 20 of this Agreement, any supplemental escrow instructions and the terms of Escrow Holder's general provisions.

Escrow Holder is advised that the date of Confirmation of Acceptance of the Agreement as between Buyer and Seller is _____

Escrow Holder _____ Escrow # _____
By _____ Date _____
Address _____
Phone/Fax/E-mail //
Escrow Holder has the following license number #
☐ Department of Business Oversight, ☐ Department of Insurance, ☐ Bureau of Real Estate.

| **PRESENTATION OF OFFER:** (_____) Listing Broker presented this offer to Seller on _____ (date). |
| Broker or Designee Initials |

| **REJECTION OF OFFER:** (___)(___) ☐ No counter offer is being made. This offer was rejected by Seller on _____ (date). |
| Seller's Initials |

©1991- 2015, California Association of REALTORS®, Inc. United States copyright law (Title 17 U.S. Code) forbids the unauthorized distribution, display and reproduction of this form, or any portion thereof, by photocopy machine or any other means, including facsimile or computerized formats.
THIS FORM HAS BEEN APPROVED BY THE CALIFORNIA ASSOCIATION OF REALTORS® (C.A.R.). NO REPRESENTATION IS MADE AS TO THE LEGAL VALIDITY OR ACCURACY OF ANY PROVISION IN ANY SPECIFIC TRANSACTION. A REAL ESTATE BROKER IS THE PERSON QUALIFIED TO ADVISE ON REAL ESTATE TRANSACTIONS. IF YOU DESIRE LEGAL OR TAX ADVICE, CONSULT AN APPROPRIATE PROFESSIONAL.

Published and Distributed by: Buyer Acknowledges that page 10 is part of this Agreement (*T.N.*)(_____)
REAL ESTATE BUSINESS SERVICES, INC.   Buyer's Initials
a subsidiary of the *CALIFORNIA ASSOCIATION OF REALTORS®*
525 South Virgil Avenue, Los Angeles, California 90020   Reviewed by _____
RPA-CA REVISED 12/15 (PAGE 10 of 10)   Broker or Designee

CALIFORNIA RESIDENTIAL PURCHASE AGREEMENT (RPA-CA PAGE 10 OF 10)

図表 7-2　買手のカウンター（返答）

CALIFORNIA ASSOCIATION OF REALTORS®

BUYER COUNTER OFFER   No. 1
(C.A.R. Form BCO, 11/14)

Date **April 5, 2018**

This is a counter offer to the: X Seller Counter Offer No. **1**, Seller Multiple Counter Offer No. _____, or Other _____ ("Offer"), dated **April 3, 2018**, on property known as **1234 Sample Street, Sample, CA 90000** ("Property"), between **Taro Nippon** ("Buyer") and **John Seller** ("Seller").

1. **TERMS:** The terms and conditions of the above referenced document are accepted subject to the following:

   A. Paragraphs in the Offer that require initials by all parties, but are not initialed by all parties, are excluded from the final agreement unless specifically referenced for inclusion in paragraph 1C of this or another Counter Offer or an addendum.

   B. Unless otherwise agreed in writing, down payment and loan amount(s) will be adjusted in the same proportion as in the original Offer.

   C. **OTHER TERMS:** *1. Sales price to be $490,000.00*

   2. Due Diligence period of Section 14B to be 17 days.

   D. The following attached addenda are incorporated into this Buyer Counter offer: Addendum No. _____

2. **EXPIRATION:** This Buyer Counter Offer shall be deemed revoked and the deposits, if any, shall be returned:

   A. Unless by 5:00pm on the third Day After the date it is signed in paragraph 3 (if more than one signature then, the last signature date)(or by _____ AM _____ PM on _____ (date)) (i) it is signed in paragraph 4 by Seller and (ii) a copy of the signed Buyer Counter Offer is personally received by Buyer or _____, who is authorized to receive it.

   OR B. If Buyer withdraws it in writing (CAR Form WOO) anytime prior to Acceptance.

3. **OFFER: BUYER MAKES THIS COUNTER OFFER ON THE TERMS AND ACKNOWLEDGES RECEIPT OF A COPY.**
   Buyer   *Taro Nippon*   Taro Nippon Date **04/05/2018**

4. **ACCEPTANCE: I/WE accept the above Buyer Counter Offer (If checked   SUBJECT TO THE ATTACHED COUNTER OFFER)** and acknowledge receipt of a Copy.
   Seller   *John Seller*   John Seller Date **04/06/2018**   Time **9:00**   X AM/ PM

CONFIRMATION OF ACCEPTANCE:

(_____ / _____) (Initials) **Confirmation of Acceptance:** A Copy of Signed Acceptance was personally received by Buyer or Buyer's authorized agent as specified in paragraph 2A on (date) _____ at _____ AM/ PM. **A binding Agreement is created when a Copy of Signed Acceptance is personally received by Buyer or Buyer's authorized agent whether or not confirmed in this document.**

BCO 11/14 (PAGE 1 OF 1)

BUYER COUNTER OFFER (BCO PAGE 1 OF 1)

第7章
売買取引と契約書

図表 7-3 売手のカウンター（返答）

CALIFORNIA ASSOCIATION OF REALTORS®

SELLER COUNTER OFFER No. 1
May not be used as a multiple counter offer.
(C.A.R. Form SCO, 11/14)

Date *April 3, 2018*

This is a counter offer to the: **X** Purchase Agreement, Buyer Counter Offer No. , or Other ("Offer"), dated *April 1, 2018* , on property known as *1234 Sample Street, Sample, CA 90000* ("Property"), between *Taro Nippon* ("Buyer") and *John Seller* ("Seller").

1. **TERMS:** The terms and conditions of the above referenced document are accepted subject to the following:
   A. Paragraphs in the Offer that require initials by all parties, but are not initialed by all parties, are excluded from the final agreement unless specifically referenced for inclusion in paragraph 1C of this or another Counter Offer or an addendum.
   B. Unless otherwise agreed in writing, down payment and loan amount(s) will be adjusted in the same proportion as in the original Offer.
   C. **OTHER TERMS:** *1. Sales price to be $495,000.00*

   2. Due Diligence time period of Section 14B to be 10 days after Acceptance.

   3. Escrow to be First American Title Escrow, and the title company First American Title Company.

   D. The following attached addenda are incorporated into this Seller Counter offer: Addendum No.

2. **EXPIRATION:** This Seller Counter Offer shall be deemed revoked and the deposits, if any, shall be returned:
   A. Unless by 5:00pm on the third Day After the date it is signed in paragraph 4 (if more than one signature then, the last signature date)(or by AM PM on (date)) (i) it is signed in paragraph 5 by Buyer and (ii) a copy of the signed Seller Counter Offer is personally received by Seller or , who is authorized to receive it.
   OR B. If Seller withdraws it anytime prior to Acceptance (CAR Form WOO may be used).
   OR C. If Seller accepts another offer prior to Buyer's Acceptance of this counter offer.

3. **MARKETING TO OTHER BUYERS:** Seller has the right to continue to offer the Property for sale. Seller has the right to accept any other offer received, prior to Acceptance of this Counter Offer by Buyer as specified in 2A and 5. In such event, Seller is advised to withdraw this Seller Counter Offer before accepting another offer.

4. **OFFER: SELLER MAKES THIS COUNTER OFFER ON THE TERMS ABOVE AND ACKNOWLEDGES RECEIPT OF A COPY.**
   Seller *John Seller* *John Seller* Date *04/03/2018*
   Seller Date

5. **ACCEPTANCE:** I/WE accept the above Seller Counter Offer (**If checked** SUBJECT TO THE ATTACHED COUNTER OFFER) and acknowledge receipt of a Copy.
   Buyer *Taro Nippon* Date Time AM/ PM
   Buyer Date Time AM/ PM

CONFIRMATION OF ACCEPTANCE:

(____ / ____) (Initials) **Confirmation of Acceptance:** A Copy of Signed Acceptance was personally received by Seller, or Seller's authorized agent as specified in paragraph 2A on (date) at AM/ PM **A binding Agreement is created when a Copy of Signed Acceptance is personally received by Seller or Seller's authorized agent whether or not confirmed in this document.**

© 2014, California Association of REALTORS®, Inc.
THIS FORM HAS BEEN APPROVED BY THE CALIFORNIA ASSOCIATION OF REALTORS® (C.A.R.). NO REPRESENTATION IS MADE AS TO THE LEGAL VALIDITY OR ACCURACY OF ANY PROVISION IN ANY SPECIFIC TRANSACTION. A REAL ESTATE BROKER IS THE PERSON QUALIFIED TO ADVISE ON REAL ESTATE TRANSACTIONS. IF YOU DESIRE LEGAL OR TAX ADVICE, CONSULT AN APPROPRIATE PROFESSIONAL.

Published and Distributed by:
REAL ESTATE BUSINESS SERVICES, INC.
a subsidiary of the California Association of REALTORS®
525 South Virgil Avenue, Los Angeles, California 90020 Reviewed by Date

SCO 11/14 (PAGE 1 OF 1)

SELLER COUNTER OFFER (SCO PAGE 1 OF 1)

Cosmo Investment 1512 Artesia Blvd., Suite 250-D, Redondo Beach, CA 90278   Phone: 310.782.4657   Fax: 1234 Sample St
Norio Kasai   Produced with zipForm® by zipLogix 18070 Fifteen Mile Road, Fraser, Michigan 48026   www.zipLogix.com

図表 7-4 オファーから合意までの経緯

1　オファー
　　価格：48万ドル、エスクロー期間：30日、デューデリジェンス（検査）期間：21日間、Chicago Title エスクロー、Chicago Title タイトル会社、など。
2　売手からのカウンター
　　価格：49.5万ドル、デューデリジェンス（検査）期間：10日間、First American Title エスクロー、First American Title 会社。
3　買手からのカウンター
　　価格：49万ドル、デューデリジェンス（検査）期間：17日間

[合意内容]

価格：49万ドル
デューデリジェンス（検査）期間：17日間
エスクロー：First American Title エスクロー
タイトル会社：First American Title 会社
エスクロー期間：30日

　以上のとおりとなり、上記の内容で合意に至ることになり、同時にエスクローがオープンします。この日から30日間でエスクローが終了、締結することになります。

ここまでのオファーから交渉、合意までの経緯を簡単にまとめますと、図表7－4のようになります。

エスクローがオープンしますと、すぐに物件の検査を専門のInspector（検査人）に依頼することになります。検査報告書は、検査後1日から3日後までにあがってきます。この検査で万一根本的な欠陥問題が指摘されますと、購入を避けたほうが良いことになり、この理由をもって契約自体をキャンセル解約することになります。

エスクローがオープンして3営業日以内に手付金、通常価格の3％をエスクロー指定の銀行口座に送金しなければいけませんが、条件内に契約をキャンセル、解約する場合は、この手付金は戻ってきます。

「条件内」というのはしかるべき理由で、デューデリジェンス（検査）期間内にキャンセルする場合です。つまり検査期間を過ぎてキャンセルする場合は、いかなる理由があっても、この手付金は戻ってきません。ただし、売主の契約不履行があれば別ですが……。

だからこそこのデューデリジェンス（検査）期間の日数が重要になってくるのです。売主はできるだけ早く売却したいので、この検査期間を短く要求してきますが、買手はじっくりと検査・調査したいため、できるだけ長くしたいということで、デューデリジェンス

期間の日数が合意に至る大事な条件のひとつになります。

物件検査で欠陥問題がない限り、傷んでいるところや修理の必要があることを売手に依頼します。当然売主は、できる限り修理をしない方向で合意を目指しますが、買手はすべての修繕を望みます。どこまで修理する・しないの交渉をデューデリジェンス期間までに合意しなければいけません。最終的には、検査レポートで「修理・手当てしておかなければいけない項目は、必ず修理する」ということで決着をつけます。

また、カリフォルニア州の木造物件ではシロアリの問題が必ずありますので、これを売主負担で検査し、結果のうち「Section 1」と呼ばれる緊急項目は、売主負担で修繕します。この点はオファー書類の第7項「ALLOCATION OF COSTS」(費用配分)の「A(2)」で シロアリ検査費用は売主負担、および「A(8)」で「Section 1」コストは売主負担としています。

デューデリジェンス(検査)期間で他に検査チェックすることは、現オーナーである売主のタイトル状態、滞っている固定資産税がないか、自然環境災害書レポートに問題はないか、などがあります。実際にはエージェントに確認してもらいます。

以上問題がなければ、残金をエスクロー締結日の3日前までにエスクロー指定銀行口座に送金します。

第7章
売買取引と契約書

「なぜエスクロー締結日の3日前までに送金しなければいけないのか？ エスクロー締結日当日に着金すればよいのでは？」とよく尋ねられますが、まず「エスクロー締結日」というのは、エスクローが準備した書類などすべてが整い、タイトル会社の担当者が、「エスクロー締結日」当日に郡当局に行き、所有権の移転・譲渡を登録するからです。この所有権の譲渡が完了して、初めてエスクローが締結することになります。そのためにはエスクロー担当者は、売主からの所有権譲渡証書完了など確かめたうえ、買手からの残金入金を確認し、また売買契約書やカウンター書類、その他修理合意書などをすべてチェックして、タイトル会社担当者に必要書類を手渡し、所有権譲渡・移転を郡当局に登録するのです。つまり、登録する前に残金も入金されていないといけないからです。

所有権が買手に譲渡・移転されて買手が物件のオーナーになります。

2 エスクロー

ここでエスクローについて述べたいと思います。

エスクローは第三者の預託者で中立を保つとされていますが、実はそうでもないのです。もちろん契約上のことはきちんとしますが、エスクローを選んでくれた側のエージェントにいろいろと便宜を図ります。たとえば相手側の動きや状況を教えたりして、取引を有利に運ぶこともあるのです。商習慣上、エスクローとタイトル会社が決めることになっていますが、法律で決まっていませんので、実際は交渉できるのです。ちなみにタイトル会社も同様です。

物件を購入しますと、物件の管理が必要になります。物件管理専門会社やエージェントに物件管理を依頼・委託することになり、その契約を締結しなければいけません。その物件管理契約書（図表7-5）と要点のまとめを付けました。ご参照ください。

物件管理費用ですが、物件の大きさ・戸数によって異なります。

第7章
売買取引と契約書

コンドミニアムやタウンハウス、一軒家の1戸物件の1か月の物件管理費用は、家賃の6％ないしは200ドル以上ですが、2戸物件は単純に200ドル×2の400ドルではなく、少し割安の350ドル（1戸当たり175ドル）と戸数が増えると少しずつ1戸分割安になります。

集合住宅のアパートになりますと、家賃の3％から5％が相場です。たとえば100部屋以上の大型アパートになりますと3％、10戸のアパートでは4・5％から5％が一般的です。

まとめますと、図表7-6のようになります。

物件管理で一番大事なことは管理費用ではなく、いかにきちんと管理をしてくれるかに尽きます。管理費用をケチって修理費用が増加したり、テナント対応に支障をきたして、かえって経費がかさめば何にもなりません。**良心的な信頼できる管理会社・エージェントを確保することが管理で最も大事なことです。**

日本の海外不動産コンサルティングでは、物件管理の他に資産管理のアドバイスも含まれますので、この物件管理費用とは別に、資産管理費用が必要になります。

物件管理は、家賃の受取り、水道代など必要な光熱費・HOA費の支払い、修繕が必要

（206ページに続く）

199

_____（以下「オーナー」）と_____
_____（以下「ブローカー」）は、下記合意する。

1. ブローカー指名：オーナーは下記物件の賃貸、管理業務をブローカー（以下「マネージャー」）独占的に任せるものとする。
   物件：_____
   期間は、_____年_____月_____日より開始、_____年_____月_____日午後 11 時 59 分に終了する。
   当初の本期間が終了すると、一方から 30 日の解約通知書がもう一方に送付されない限り継続するものとする。

2. マネージャー受諾：マネージャーは指名を受け、A：本契約の内容の調査・分析、B：物件の賃貸および管理業務、を合意する。

3. 権限と執行力：オーナーは、オーナー負担で下記事項ついてブローカーに権限を与える。
   A. 広告：賃貸・リース中のサインを付けたり、MLS に物件の新テナント賃貸募集をする。
   B. 賃貸：賃貸契約書を実行、それに伴い敷金、家賃などを受領。契約は 1 年を上限とし、家賃は相場相当とする。
   C. 賃貸契約解約：賃貸契約を解除・解約し、テナント退去手続きを行う。
   D. 修繕・維持：必要に応じ修繕など行う。修繕費が_____ドルを超える場合は、事前にオーナーの承諾を取る。
   E. 通知・サイン：連邦、州、市の法律に従って通知などを行う。
   F. 契約（サービス）：物件管理業務に必要に応じて、弁護士を含む各業者と契約をする。
   G. 費用支払い：必要な費用支払いを行う。
   H. 敷金：敷金はオーナーに支払うか、マネージャーのトラスト口座で預かる。
   I. トラスト金：家賃から必要経費を差し引いた金額を銀行トラスト口座に入金する。
   J. 準備積立金：マネージャーのトラスト口座に_____ドル準備金を維持する。
   K. 支払い：マネージャーのトラスト口座のオーナーの資金から次の順序で支払いをする。
      (K.1) 下記第 8 条項のマネージャーへの支払い。
      (K.2) 管理業務運営必要経費。
      (K.3) 敷金および積み立て準備金
      (K.4) オーナーへの残額（ネット金額）

図表 7-5 物件管理契約書

日付　　物件管理契約書（一部要訳）

PROPERTY MANAGEMENT AGREEMENT
(C.A.R. Form PMA, Revised 6/17)

CALIFORNIA ASSOCIATION OF REALTORS®

Date Prepared: *May 7, 2018*

Taro Nippon ("Owner"), and
ABC Property Management Company ("Broker"), agree as follows:

1. **APPOINTMENT OF BROKER:** Owner hereby appoints and grants Broker (hereinafter "Property Manager") the exclusive right to rent, lease, operate and manage the property(ies) known as *1234 Sample Street, Sample, CA 90000* and any additional property that may later be added to this Agreement ("Property"), upon the terms below, for the period beginning (date) *May 7, 2018* and ending (date) *May 6, 2019*, at 11:59 PM. (If checked:) ☐ Either party may terminate this Property Management Agreement ("Agreement") on at least 30 days written notice ______ months after the original commencement date of this Agreement. After the exclusive term expires, this Agreement shall continue as a non-exclusive agreement that either party may terminate by giving at least 30 days written notice to the other.
2. **PROPERTY MANAGER ACCEPTANCE:** Property Manager accepts the appointment and grant, and agrees to:
   - A. Use due diligence in the performance of this Agreement.
   - B. Furnish the services of its firm for the rental, leasing, operation and management of the Property.
3. **AUTHORITY AND POWERS:** Owner grants Property Manager the authority and power, at Owner's expense, to:
   - A. **ADVERTISING:** Display FOR RENT/LEASE and similar signs on the Property. Advertise the availability of the Property, or any part thereof, for rental or lease in the Multiple Listing Service and other online media.
   - B. **RENTAL; LEASING:** Initiate, sign, renew, modify or cancel rental agreements and leases for the Property, or any part thereof; collect and give receipts for rents, other fees, charges and security deposits. Any lease or rental agreement executed by Property Manager for Owner shall not exceed ___ year(s) or ☐ shall be month-to-month. Unless Owner authorizes a lower amount, rent shall be: ☒ at market rate; OR ☐ a minimum of $ ______ per ______ ; OR ☐ see attachment.
   - C. **TENANCY TERMINATION:** Sign and serve in Owner's name notices that are required or appropriate; commence and prosecute actions to evict tenants; recover possession of the Property in Owner's name; recover rents and other sums due; and, when expedient, settle, compromise and release claims, actions and suits and/or reinstate tenancies. If Landlord permits Tenant to pay rent by direct deposit such as wire or electronic transfer or other online method, Landlord should discuss with a Landlord-Tenant attorney the implications of doing so in the event Tenant defaults and an eviction becomes necessary.
   - D. **REPAIR; MAINTENANCE:** Make, cause to be made, and/or supervise repairs, improvements, alterations and decorations to the Property; purchase, and pay bills for, services and supplies. Owner agrees that state and local water use restrictions will supersede any obligation by Property Manager or any Tenant to water/maintain gardens, landscaping trees or shrubs. Property Manager shall obtain prior approval of Owner for all expenditures over $ *500.00* for any one item. Prior approval shall not be required for monthly or recurring operating charges or, if in Property Manager's opinion, emergency expenditures over the maximum are needed to protect the Property or other property(ies) from damage, prevent injury to persons, avoid suspension of necessary services, avoid penalties or fines, or suspension of services to tenants required by a lease or rental agreement or by law, including, but not limited to, maintaining the Property in a condition fit for human habitation as required by Civil Code §§ 1941 and 1941.1 and Health and Safety Code §§ 17920.3 and 17920.10.
   - E. **REPORTS, NOTICES AND SIGNS:** Comply with federal, state or local law requiring delivery of reports or notices and/or posting of signs or notices.
   - F. **CONTRACTS; SERVICES:** Contract, hire, supervise and/or discharge firms and persons, including utilities, required for the operation and maintenance of the Property. Property Manager may perform any of Property Manager's duties through attorneys, agents, employees, or independent contractors and, except for persons working in Property Manager's firm, shall not be responsible for their acts, omissions, defaults, negligence and/or costs of same.
   - G. **EXPENSE PAYMENTS:** Pay expenses and costs for the Property from Owner's funds held by Property Manager, unless otherwise directed by Owner. Expenses and costs may include, but are not limited to, property management compensation, fees and charges, expenses for goods and services, property taxes and other taxes, Owner's Association dues, assessments, loan payments and insurance premiums
   - H. **SECURITY DEPOSITS:** Receive security deposits from tenants, which deposits shall be ☐ given to Owner, or ☐ placed in Property Manager's trust account and, if held in Property Manager's trust account, pay from Owner's funds all interest on tenants' security deposits if required by local law or ordinance. Owner shall be responsible to tenants for return of security deposits and all interest due on security deposits held by Owner.
   - I. **TRUST FUNDS:** Deposit all receipts collected for Owner, less any sums properly deducted or disbursed, in a financial institution whose deposits are insured by an agency of the United States government. The funds shall be held in a trust account separate from Property Manager's personal accounts. Property Manager shall not be liable in event of bankruptcy or failure of a financial institution.
   - J. **RESERVES:** Maintain a reserve in Property Manager's trust account of $ *500.00*
   - K. **DISBURSEMENTS:** Disburse Owner's funds held in Property Manager's trust account in the following order:
     - (1) Compensation due Property Manager under paragraph 8.
     - (2) All other operating expenses, costs and disbursements payable from Owner's funds held by Property Manager.
     - (3) Reserves and security deposits held by Property Manager.
     - (4) Balance to Owner.

Owner's Initials (.........) (.........)

PMA REVISED 6/17 (PAGE 1 OF 4)

PROPERTY MANAGEMENT AGREEMENT (PMA PAGE 1 OF 4)

Cosmo Investment 2512 Artesia Blvd., Suite 250-D, Redondo Beach, CA 90278 　Phone: 310.782.4657　Fax:　1234 Sample St
Norio Kanai　Produced with zipForm® by zipLogix 18070 Fifteen Mile Road, Fraser, Michigan 48026 www.zipLogix.com

E.（　）シロアリ駆除：オーナーは定期的なシロアリ駆除の契約を締結しており、その通知をマネージャーに提出する。
F.（　）メタンガス汚染：当局からメタンガス汚染の通知があって、オーナーは除去（　）した。（　）していない。
G. ベッド南京虫開示：オーナーは2017年1月1日から2018年1月1日までの新しいテナントには定型フォームBBDにてベッド南京虫の開示をしなければならない。
H.（　）副水道メーター：2戸以上がひとつの水道管で水道供給がなされている場合、オーナーは副メーターを付けて各部屋の使用量に応じて水道代を請求できる。2018年1月1日より、規制によりオーナーはマネージャーに定型フォームを付けるようにする。
I.（　）家主は二酸化炭素報知器を付けている、（　）付けていない。
J.（　）火災煙報知器を各部屋に付けている、（　）付けていない。
K. 節水器具：トイレなど節水用の器具を付けている、（　）付けていない。
L. 湯沸かし器：湯沸かし器は倒れにくくするため、きちんと
M. 提案65（汚染水の吸飲）：オーナーは提案65の警告を貼っている（　）貼っていない。

8. 報酬：
  A. オーナーは、下記示された金額、手数料をマネージャーに支払うものとする。
   (1) 管理：＿＿＿＿＿＿＿＿＿＿＿＿
   (2) リース：＿＿＿＿＿＿＿＿＿＿＿＿
   (3) 退去：＿＿＿＿＿＿＿＿＿＿＿＿
   (4) リース募集準備：＿＿＿＿＿＿＿＿＿
   (5) 空室期間時：＿＿＿＿＿＿＿＿＿＿
   (6) 追加およびその他サービス：＿＿＿＿＿
   (7) その他：＿＿＿＿＿＿＿＿＿＿
  B. 本契約では、オンサイト・マネージメント、セール、ローン手配、損傷の回復、税金や法的アドバイス、カウンセリングなど行わない。
  C. マネージャーは、報酬、手数料など分けることができる。
  D. オーナーは下記合意するものとする。
   (1) マネージャーは、(i) リース譲渡、サブリース、(ii) クレジット申請、(iii) 遅延支払や不渡小切手、(iv) 本契約に反しないその他のサービスで、テナントからのお金を預かっておくことができる。
   (2) マネージャーは、下記関連会社や所有権保有の会社より、必要な物品やサービス提供のコミッションや一部収益を享受できる。
   ＿＿＿＿＿＿＿＿＿＿＿＿＿＿＿＿＿＿＿＿＿＿＿＿＿
   マネージャーはそのような場合、オーナーに情報公開するもの。
   (3) その他：＿＿＿＿＿＿＿＿＿＿＿＿＿＿＿＿＿＿＿

9. 代理関係：オーナーは、マネージャーがオーナーとテナントの両方の代理人となることに同意する。

10. 通知：本契約における書面による通知は、オーナー、マネージャー共、第1郵便またはお互いに合意した通知方法で下記の住所に送付するもの。通知はアメリカの郵便で投函後3日後、または（　）＿＿＿＿＿＿＿＿には、届いたものとする。

第7章
売買取引と契約書

Owner Name: Taro Nippon　　　　　　　　　　　　　　　　　　　　　　　　　　Date: **May 7, 2018**

　　Owner has no reports or records pertaining to asbestos in the Property, except:
　　Owner has no knowledge of asbestos currently in the Property, except:

E. **PEST CONTROL:** Owner has entered into a contract for periodic pest control treatment of the Property. Owner, within 3 days, will provide Property Manager a copy of the notice originally given to owner by the pest control company.

F. **METH CONTAMINATION:** Owner has received an order from a health official prohibiting occupancy of any part of the Property because of methamphetamine contamination. Owner, within 3 days, will provide Property Manager a copy of the order. Contamination specified in the order ☐ has or ☐ has not been remediated.

G. **BED BUG DISCLOSURE:** Owner acknowledges that beginning July 1, 2017, for new tenants and by January 1, 2018, all tenants must be provided a notice regarding bed bugs (C.A.R. Form BBD). Owner further acknowledges that it is unlawful to show, rent, or lease a property if there is a known current bed bug infestation. ☐ Owner knows of a current infestation.

H. **WATER SUBMETERS:** The Property contains two or more units served by a single water meter and Owner has installed a submeter to measure and charge each individual unit for water usage. Effective January 1, 2018, Owner agrees to comply with Civil Code §§ 1954.201 through 1954.219 and authorizes Property Manager to provide the required Water Submeter Addendum (C.A.R. Form WSM).

I. **CARBON MONOXIDE DETECTORS:** The Premises has a fossil fuel burning heater, appliance, or an attached garage. Landlord has ☐ has not installed carbon monoxide detector devices in accordance with legal requirements.

J. **SMOKE ALARMS:** Owner has ☐ has not installed smoke alarm(s) in each bedroom, in the hallway outside of each bedroom and on each floor whether or not a bedroom is located on the floor in compliance with legal requirements.

K. **WATER CONSERVING PLUMBING FIXTURES:** The Premises was built prior to January 1, 1994. The Owner has ☐ has not installed water conserving fixtures (toilets, shower heads, interior faucets, urinals) as per Civil Code section 1101.1 et seq effective as of 1/1/2017 for single family residential properties and 1/1/2019 for multifamily residential properties.

L. **WATER HEATERS:** Water heater has ☐ has not been braced, anchored or strapped to resist falling or horizontal displacement due to earthquake motion.

M. **PROP. 65 WARNING NOTICE:** Owner has ☐ has not posted a Proposition 65 warning notice on the Property.

8. **COMPENSATION:**

A. Owner agrees to pay Property Manager fees in the amounts indicated below for
(1) Management: *$200.00 per month*
(2) Renting or Leasing: *6% of the annual rent*
(3) Evictions *cost plus the attorney's fee.*
(4) Preparing Property for rental or lease: *Anything not covered by the previous tenant's security deposit.*
(5) Managing Property during extended periods of vacancy:
(6) An overhead and service fee added to the cost of all work performed by, or at the direction of, Property Manager:
(7) Other:

B. This Agreement does not include providing on-site management services, property sales, refinancing, preparing Property for sale or refinancing, modernization, fire or major damage restoration, rehabilitation, obtaining income tax, accounting or legal advice, representation before public agencies, advising on proposed new construction, debt collection, counseling, attending Owner's Association meetings or

If Owner requests Property Manager to perform services not included in this Agreement, a fee shall be agreed upon before these services are performed.

C. Property Manager may divide compensation, fees and charges due under this Agreement in any manner acceptable to Property Manager.

D. Owner further agrees that:
(1) Property Manager may receive and keep fees and charges from tenants for: (i) requesting an assignment of lease or sublease of the Property; (ii) processing credit applications; (iii) any returned checks and/or (☐ if checked) late payments; and (iv) any other services that are not in conflict with this Agreement.
(2) Property Manager may perform any of Property Manager's duties, and obtain necessary products and services, through affiliated companies or organizations in which Property Manager may own an interest. Property Manager may receive fees, commissions and/or profits from these affiliated companies or organizations. Property Manager has an ownership interest in the following affiliated companies or organizations:

Property Manager shall disclose to Owner any other such relationships as they occur. Property Manager shall not receive any fees, commissions or profits from unaffiliated companies or organizations in the performance of this Agreement, without prior disclosure to Owner.
(3) Other:

9. **AGENCY RELATIONSHIPS:** Property Manager may act, and Owner hereby consents to Property Manager acting, as dual agent for Owner and tenant(s) in any resulting transaction. If the Property includes residential property with one-to-four dwelling units and this Agreement permits a tenancy in excess of one year, Owner acknowledges receipt of the "Disclosure Regarding Agency Relationships" (C.A.R. Form AD). Owner understands that Property Manager may have or obtain property management agreements on other property, and that potential tenants may consider, make offers on, or lease through Property Manager, property the same as or similar to Owner's Property. Owner consents to Property Manager's representation of other owners' properties before, during and after the expiration of this Agreement.

10. **NOTICES:** Any written notice to Owner or Property Manager required under this Agreement shall be served by sending such notice by first class mail or other agreed-to delivery method to that party at the address below, or at any different address the parties may later designate for this purpose. Notice shall be deemed received three (3) calendar days after deposit into the United States mail OR

Owner's Initials (____) (____)

PMA REVISED 6/17 (PAGE 3 OF 4)
PROPERTY MANAGEMENT AGREEMENT (PMA PAGE 3 OF 4)

11. 論争解決:
   A. 第3者調停:オーナー、マネージャー共に調停することに合意する。
   B. 追加調停事項:下記事項は調停より除外される。
      (i) 抵当権流れ
      (ii) 不法占拠
      (iii) メカニック権（建築費用未払い請求権）
      (iv) 破産など。
   C. 諮問忠告:オーナー、マネージャー共法廷で争わない場合、定型フォーム ARB を締結することができる。

12. 連邦、州、地方自治体の反差別各法に基づいている。

13. 弁護士費用:訴訟敗者は弁護士費用を負担。11A 項目は除く。

14. 追加事項:(　) ロックボックス定型フォーム KLA；(　) 鉛ペイント定型フォーム FLD
_____

15. 時間の重要性；契約全体；変更:時間は重要である。本契約は最終的かつ完全で前契約や口頭での取交しがあっても及ばない。本契約上に有効でない条項があってもその他の条項が優先する。また、本契約の変更や延長は書面によるものとする。本契約、追加書類、添付書類はすべてそのコピーも含めてひとつの書類群とみなす。オーナーは、当該物件の所有者であるか、または本契約を執行する権限を有することを保証する。オーナーは本契約書を読み理解し受諾しコピーを受領したとする。

(　) 代理者範囲:本契約書はオーナーの代理者が定型フォーム RCSD-LL でもって署名しうるとする。本契約書ならびにその他の関連する書類の署名とイニシャルはこの代理者の許容範囲内である。オーナーは、(i) 署名者の法人は実在することを表し、(ii) 権限実行の証明とともに本契約を署名・執行してから 3 日以内にブローカーに手渡す。

```
オーナー_____  日付_____
        名前_____  納税者番号_____
住所:_____
電話番号:_____FAX_____Email_____
オーナー_____  日付_____
        名前_____  納税者番号_____
住所:_____
電話番号:_____FAX_____Email_____
不動産ブローカー(社名)_____  免許番号_____
エージェント_____  免許番号_____
住所:_____
電話番号:_____FAX_____Email_____
```

第7章
売買取引と契約書

Owner Name: **Taro Nippon** Date: **May 7, 2018**

11. DISPUTE RESOLUTION:

A. **MEDIATION:** Owner and Property Manager agree to mediate any dispute or claim arising between them out of this Agreement, or any resulting transaction before resorting to arbitration or court action. Mediation fees, if any, shall be divided equally among the parties involved. If, for any dispute or claim to which this paragraph applies, any party (i) commences an action without first attempting to resolve the matter through mediation, or (ii) before commencement of an action, refuses to mediate after a request has been made, then that party shall not be entitled to recover attorney fees, even if they would otherwise be available to that party in any such action.Exclusions from this mediation agreement are specified in paragraph 11B.

B. **ADDITIONAL MEDIATION TERMS:** The following matters shall be excluded from mediation and arbitration: (i) a judicial or non-judicial foreclosure or other action or proceeding to enforce a deed of trust, mortgage or installment land sale contract as defined in Civil Code §2985; (ii) an unlawful detainer action; (iii) the filing or enforcement of a mechanic's lien; and (iv) any matter that is within the jurisdiction of a probate, small claims or bankruptcy court. The filing of a court action to enable the recording of a notice of pending action, for order of attachment, receivership, injunction, or other provisional remedies, shall not constitute a waiver or violation of the mediation provisions.

C. **ADVISORY:** If Owner and Property Manager desire to resolve disputes arising between them rather than court, they can document their agreement by attaching and signing an Arbitration Agreement (C.A.R. Form ARB).

12. EQUAL HOUSING OPPORTUNITY: The Property is offered in compliance with federal, state and local anti-discrimination laws.

13. ATTORNEY FEES: In any action, proceeding or arbitration between Owner and Property Manager to enforce the compensation provisions of this Agreement, the prevailing Owner or Property Manager shall be entitled to reasonable attorney fees and costs from the non-prevailing Owner or Property Manager, except as provided in paragraph 11A.

14. ADDITIONAL TERMS: ☐ Keysafe/Lockbox Addendum (C.A.R. Form KLA); ☐ Lead-Based Paint and Lead-Based Paint Hazards Disclosure (C.A.R. Form FLD)

15. TIME OF ESSENCE; ENTIRE CONTRACT; CHANGES: Time is of the essence. All understandings between the parties are incorporated in this Agreement. Its terms are intended by the parties as a final, complete and exclusive expression of their Agreement with respect to its subject matter, and may not be contradicted by evidence of any prior agreement or contemporaneous oral agreement. If any provision of this Agreement is held to be ineffective or invalid, the remaining provisions will nevertheless be given full force and effect. Neither this Agreement nor any provision in it may be extended, amended, modified, altered or changed except in writing. This Agreement and any supplement, addendum or modification, including any copy, may be signed in two or more counterparts, all of which shall constitute one and the same writing.

Owner warrants that Owner is the owner of the Property or has the authority to execute this Agreement. Owner acknowledges Owner has read, understands, accepts and has received a copy of the Agreement.

☐ REPRESENTATIVE CAPACITY: This Property Management Agreement is being signed for Owner by an individual acting in a Representative Capacity as specified in the attached Representative Capacity Signature Disclosure (C.A.R. Form RCSD-LL). Wherever the signature or initials of the representative identified in the RCSD appear on this Agreement or any related documents, it shall be deemed to be in a representative capacity for the entity described and not in an individual capacity, unless otherwise indicated. Owner (i) represents that the entity for which the individual is signing already exists and (ii) shall Deliver to Broker, within 3 Days After Execution of this Agreement, evidence of authority to act (such as but not limited to: applicable trust document, or portion thereof, letters testamentary, court order, power of attorney, corporate resolution, or formation documents of the business entity).

Owner Date **05/07/2018**
Owner **Taro Nippon**
Print Name Social Security/Tax ID # (for tax reporting purposes)
Address City State Zip
Telephone Fax Email

Owner Date
Owner
Print Name Social Security/Tax ID # (for tax reporting purposes)
Address City State Zip
Telephone Fax Email

Real Estate Broker (Firm) **ABC Property Management Company** Cal BRE Lic. #:
By (Agent) Cal BRE Lic. # Date **05/07/2018**
Address City State **CA** Zip
Telephone Fax Email

© 1991-2017, California Association of REALTORS®, Inc. United States copyright law (Title 17 U.S. Code) forbids the unauthorized distribution, display and reproduction of this form, or any portion thereof, by photocopy machine or any other means, including facsimile or computerized formats.
THIS FORM HAS BEEN APPROVED BY THE CALIFORNIA ASSOCIATION OF REALTORS®. NO REPRESENTATION IS MADE AS TO THE LEGAL VALIDITY OR ACCURACY OF ANY SPECIFIC PROVISION IN ANY SPECIFIC TRANSACTION. A REAL ESTATE BROKER IS THE PERSON QUALIFIED TO ADVISE ON REAL ESTATE TRANSACTIONS. IF YOU DESIRE LEGAL OR TAX ADVICE, CONSULT AN APPROPRIATE PROFESSIONAL.

Published and Distributed by:
REAL ESTATE BUSINESS SERVICES, INC.
a subsidiary of the California Association of REALTORS®
525 South Virgil Avenue, Los Angeles, California 90020

Reviewed by _____ Date _____

PMA REVISED 6/17 (PAGE 4 OF 4)

PROPERTY MANAGEMENT AGREEMENT (PMA PAGE 4 OF 4)

図表7-6 管理費用の目安(1カ月)

1戸物件 (コンドミニアム、タウンハウス、一軒家)	6% ないしは200ドル
2戸物件 (Duplex)	350ドル
3戸物件 (Triplex)	450ドル
4戸物件 (Fourplex)	500ドル
5戸以上の物件。	3%〜5% (戸数が多くなれば なるほど%は下がる)

[2017年12月現在]

(199ページから続く)

になった場合の手配・費用支払いなどになります。

これに対し資産管理は、賃料の相場チェックと進言、資産価値を高めるリフォームや外壁のペイントなどなど、単なる家賃徴収・費用支払いに限定される物件管理以上のことをアドバイスすることです。

3 不動産手数料

本章の最後にアメリカの不動産手続料について述べたいと思います。

その前にアメリカの不動産ビジネスは、ひとつのしっかりしたビジネス業務で、法律で明確になっています。ひとつの事業として確立されていて、奇奇怪怪・怪しげな裏取引など全くあり得ません。すべて法律に基づいていますので、おかしなことはできないのです。

また不動産エージェントは、どんな大きな不動産会社に所属していても、すべて個人事業主です。日本のような給与所得者ではないのです。所属している不動産会社にロイアリティー（またはフランチャイズフィー）を支払って、自分で顧客を探し取引を完了しなければ、報酬は一切ありません。取引が成立しても所属不動産会社にフィーを支払い、すべて出来高払いになります。

不動産手数料ですが、100％売主が支払い、そのフィーは取扱物件の売買価格により決まります。例外はありますが、通常の相場を**図表7-7**に掲げました。

図表 7-7 不動産手数料 [一般的相場]

物件価格	
200万ドル〜300万ドル以下	5%
300万ドル〜500万ドル	4%
500万ドル〜1,000万ドル	3%〜3.5%
1,000万ドル以上	2%〜3%
2,000万ドル以上	2%以下

あくまでも目安ですので、売主とエージェント間の交渉次第ですが、あまり厳しく交渉しますとやる気をなくしてしまいます。ここは頑張ってもらうために、相場かそれ以上の手数料を出したほうが効率的と思います。不動産は売れなければ絵に描いた餅ですし、手数料は経費で落ちますから。

実際は、売主のエージェントと買手のエージェントがその手数料を折半します。

買手が手数料を支払う必要は一切ありませんが、購入後物件を売却する時は、自分が売手になるわけですから、全額支払うことになります。

補章

物件・案件の紹介

節税に最適の物件（物件1から7まで）、売却益が見込まれるリフォーム改装案件（物件8から12まで）を、ご紹介致します。

物件1

住所：224 Bayview Drive, Hermosa Beach, CA 90254

物件内容		運営支出（推定）	
価格	$ 1,359,000	固定資産税(1.25%)	17,362
戸数	2	保険	900
建物面積(s.f., m2)	1,080　　99m2	管理費($350/mo)	4,200
土地面積(s.f., m2)	1,499　　137m2	AM費	
築年	1947	修理・維持費	600
建物比率	24%→70%	電気	600
償却額（4年）	972,300㌦ (70%)	ガス	0
CAP(推定ネット利回り) ＊	2.27%(1), 2.62%(2)	水道	1,800
年間償却額 ($1=110円) 1年	2,673万円	ゴミ	360
1戸当り価格	$ 694,500	ランドスケーピング	
NOI	$ 30,905(1), 35,633(2)	その他	600
取得費用（推定）	約24,500㌦	合計（全改装後）	$ 26,422

収入			各戸内訳			
賃料	58,200(1)	63,000(2)	戸数	タイプ　現賃料	1	2
空室率(1.5%)	▲873	▲945	1	2bd-1ba （空き） 2,850	3,000㌦	
			1	1bd-1ba 1,750	2,000	2,250㌦
合計	57,327	62,055		1,750㌦	4,850㌦	5,250㌦

コメント	ロケーションはA−〜A。ビーチへ徒歩圏内で、トレンディーなレストランやお店などが立ち並ぶメインストリートにも近い。2Bedは改装済みで空きのため新しいテナントを募集するが、相場は3,000㌦前後。1Bedの賃貸契約は月決めのため、購入後2か月通知で賃料値上げ可能。

補章
物件・案件紹介

物件2

住所：607 8th Place, Hermosa Beach, CA 90254

物件内容			運営支出（推定）	
価格	$ 1,475,000		固定資産税(1.25%)	18,437
戸数	2		保険	1,000
建物面積(s.f., m2)	1,568	144m2	管理費($350/mo)	4,200
土地面積(s.f., m2)	2,782	255m2	AM費	
築年	1954		修理・維持費	600
建物比率	38%→70%		電気	200
償却額（4年）	1,032,500 ﾄﾞﾙ (70%)		ガス	300
CAP(推定ネット利回り) ＊	2.8%(1), 3.2%(2)		水道	1,000
年間償却額 ($1=110円) 1年	2,839万円		ゴミ	360
1戸当り価格	$ 737,500		ランドスケーピング	
NOI	$ 41,268(1), 47,178(2)		その他	600
取得費用（推定）	約25,850 ﾄﾞﾙ		合計（全改装後）	$ 26,697

収入			各戸内訳			
賃料	69,000(1)	75,000(2)	戸数	タイプ 現賃料	1	2
空室率(1.5%)	▲1,035	▲1,125	1	2bd-1ba（空き） 3,500 ﾄﾞﾙ		3,750 ﾄﾞﾙ
			1	1bd-1ba 1,500 ﾄﾞﾙ 2,250 ﾄﾞﾙ		2,500 ﾄﾞﾙ
合計	67,965	73,875	2	1,500 ﾄﾞﾙ 5,750 ﾄﾞﾙ		6,250 ﾄﾞﾙ

コメント	ロケーションはA−〜A。ビーチまで徒歩圏内で、すぐ近くに散歩道があり落ち着きのある街並み。1Bedの賃貸契約は月決めのため、購入後2か月通知で賃料値上げ可能。

補章
物件・案件紹介

物件3

住所:817 18th Street, Hermosa Beach, CA 90254

物件内容		運営支出(推定)	
価格	$ 1,875,000	固定資産税(1.25%)	23,737
戸数	2	保険	900
建物面積(s.f., m2)	2,400 220m2	管理費($300/mo)	3,600
土地面積(s.f., m2)	2,498 229m2	AM費	
築年	1973	修理・維持費	600
建物比率	67%	電気	200
償却額(4年)	1,272,330ドル	ガス	300
CAP(推定ネット利回り) *	4.08%	水道	1,000
年間償却額 ($1=110円) 1年	3,498万円	ゴミ	360
1戸当り価格	$ 949,500	ランドスケーピング	
NOI	$ 76,583	その他	600
取得費用(推定)	約33,500ドル	合計(全改装後)	$ 31,297

収入		各戸内訳		
		戸数	タイプ	現賃料
賃料	107,880	2	3bd-2ba	4,695ドル 4,295ドル
空室率(現在満室)				
合計	107,880			8,990ドル

コメント	ロケーションはA−。物件所在地は坂の途中にあり、2階からはオーシャンヴィュー。2戸とも上下のメゾネット式で人気がある。両室とも充分な家賃が取れており、CAP4%を達成。

補章
物件・案件紹介

補章
物件・案件紹介

物件4

住所：5540 Kinston Ave., Culver City, CA 90230

物件内容			運営支出（推定）	
価格	$ 1,700,000		固定資産税(1.25%)	21,250
戸数	4		保険	1,275
建物面積(s.f., m2)	3,160	290m2	管理費($450/mo)	5,400
土地面積(s.f., m2)	5,728	526m2	AM 費	
築年	1951		修理・維持費	6,500
建物比率	40%→75%		電気・ガス・水道	2,550
償却額（4年）	1,275,00万円 (75%)			
CAP(推定ネット利回り) ＊	3.83%, 4.5%(1)			
年間償却額 ($1=110円) 1年	3,506万円		ゴミ	600
1戸当り価格	$ 425,000		ランドスケーピング	
NOI	$ 65,165, 76,438(1)		その他	1,000
取得費用（推定）	約29,750万円		合計（全改装後）	$ 38,575

収入			各戸内訳			
賃料	103,740	117,360(1)	戸数	タイプ	現賃料	値上げ後 1
空室率(2%)	(満室)	▲2,347	2	2bd-1.5ba	2150,2495	2,495万円, 2,495万円
			2	2bd-1ba	1950,2050	2,395万円, 2,395万円
合計	103,740	115,013	4		8,645万円	9,780万円

コメント	ロケーションはB+〜A−。シリコンビーチに近く人気上昇中。カルバーシティーの中心。特筆すべきはレントコントロールはない。購入後、家賃値上げ可能。全室内に各洗濯機・乾燥機付き。

補章
物件・案件紹介

物件5

住所:21013 Reynolds Drive, Torrance, CA 90503

物件内容		
価格	$ 2,775,000	
戸数	8	
建物面積(s.f., m2)	4,350	400m2
土地面積(s.f., m2)	6,900	634m2
築年	1961	
建物比率	63%→75%	
償却額(4年)	2,083,500ドル (75%)	
CAP(推定ネット利回り) *	3.8%, 4.46%(1)	
年間償却額($1=110円)1年	5,729万円	
1戸当り価格	$ 347,250	
NOI	$ 105,681, 123,761(1)	
取得費用(推定)	約29,750ドル	

運営支出(推定)		
固定資産税(1.25%)	34,687	
保険	2,400	
管理費(5%)	8,362	9,290(1)
AM費		
修理・維持費	4,000	
電気	420	
ガス	2,400	
水道	3,200	
ゴミ	2,400	
ランドスケーピング	1,200	
その他(ライセンス等)	2,500	
合計(全改装後)	$ 61,569	62,497(1)

収入		
賃料	166,800	189,600(1)
空室率(2%)	(満室)	▲3,792
ランドリー	450	450
合計	167,250	186,258(1)

各戸内訳			
戸数	タイプ	現賃料	値上げ後1
8	1bd-1ba	1450~1950	1950~2000ドル
4		13,900ドル	15,800ドル

コメント	ロケーションはB+~A-。トーランスの優良学校区で人気のエリアで、レントコントロールはない。購入後、家賃値上げ可能。8戸のうち半分の4戸が改装済み。

補章
物件・案件紹介

物件6

住所：8119 Cheyenne Avenue, Downey, CA 90242

物件内容			運営支出（推定）	
価格	$ 899,000		固定資産税(1.25%)	11,237
戸数	2		保険	1,250
建物面積(s.f., m2)	3,609	332m2	管理費($350/mo)	4,200
土地面積(s.f., m2)	5,241	482m2	AM費	
築年	1990		修理・維持費	1,200
建物比率	57%→75%		電気	900
償却額（4年）	674,250㌦ (75%)		ガス	600
CAP(推定ネット利回り) *	4.3%, 4.62%(1)		水道	900
年間償却額 ($1=110円) 1年	1,854万円		ゴミ	600
1戸当り価格	$ 449,500			
NOI	$ 38,613, 41,529(1)		その他(ライセンス等)	500
取得費用（推定）	約16,000㌦		合計（全改装後）	$ 21,387

収入			各戸内訳			
賃料	60,000	64,200(1)	戸数	タイプ	現賃料	値上げ後1
空室率(2%)	(満室)	▲1,284	2	3bd-3ba	2,500㌦	2600㌦, 2750㌦
合計	60,000	62,916(1)	4		5,000㌦	5,350㌦

コメント	ロケーションはB。ロス・ダウンタウンに車で10~15分の平均的エリアで、レントコントロールはない。購入後、家賃値上げ可能。

補章
物件・案件紹介

補章
物件・案件紹介

物件7

住所：16100 Sunset Blvd., Pacific Palisades, CA 90272

物件内容		運営支出（推定）	
価格	$ 14,295,000	固定資産税(1.25%)	178,688
戸数	20	保険	12,502
建物面積(s.f., m2)	20,522　　1,888m2	管理費(3%)	20,393
土地面積(s.f., m2)	17,916　　1,648m2	AM 費	
築年	1995	修理・維持費	31,660
建物比率	31%→65%	電気,ガス,水道,ゴミ	23,791
償却額（4年）	9,291,750 ドル (65%)		
CAP(推定ネット利回り)＊	2.53%(1), 2.97%(2)	オンサイト管理人	29,940
年間償却額 ($1=110円) 1 年	2 億 5,552 万円	エレベーター	3,470
1 戸当り価格	$ 714,750	ランドスケープ	7,295
NOI	$ 362,30(1), 424,912(2)	その他(ライセンス等)	10,000
取得費用（推定）	約 250,000 ドル	合計（全改装後）	$ 317,739

収入			各戸内訳			
		戸数	タイプ		値上げ後 1	値上げ後 2
賃料	690,120 (1)　753,960 (2)	10	2bd-2ba	3500~3745 ドル		3650 ドル~3745 ドル
空室率(1.5%)	▲10,351　▲11,309	10	1bd-1ba	2500~2745 ドル		2650 ドル~2745 ドル
合計	679,769(1)　742,651 (2)	20			57,510 ドル	62,830 ドル

コメント	ロケーションは A～A+。ロスでも指折りの高級住宅地であるパシフィック・パリセーズで賃貸物件は非常に珍しく本物件はアパートというより、コンドミニアム仕様に近い。20 戸のうち 14 戸は改装済み。レントコントロールはないため、購入後家賃値上げ可能。費用面を効率的に削減すれば CAP は 3%前半に改善。

補章
物件・案件紹介

補章
物件・案件紹介

物件8

住所：2020 Arlington Avenue, Torrance, CA 90501

物件内容		
価格	$ 買939,000	(売1,450,000)
戸数	3	
建物面積(s.f., m2)	2,168	199m2
土地面積(s.f., m2)	6,376	586m2
築年	1921	
建物比率	25%→75%	
償却額（4年）	1,087,500㌦	
CAP(推定ネット利回り) ＊	2.79%(1), 3.25%(2)	
年間償却額（$1=110円）1年	2,990万円	
1戸当り価格	$ 483,333	
リノベーション費用：		
[内訳] 3Bed:6万㌦、2Bed:4万㌦、1Bed:3万㌦	$ 130,000	
NOI（全改装後）	$ 40,434(1), 46,902(2)	
取得費用（推定）	約25,000㌦	
総コスト合計＊（推定）	$ 1,154,000	(含販売手数料)

運営支出（売却$1.45M後推定）	
固定資産税(1.25%)	18,125
保険	1,800
管理費($450/mo)	5,400
AM費	
修理・維持費	900
電気	1,500
ガス	750
水道	1,500
ゴミ	750
ランドスケーピング	780
ライセンス	73
その他	900
合計（全改装後）	$ 32,478

収入				各戸内訳			
			戸数	タイプ	現賃料	改装後1	2
賃料	45,120	74,400(1)	81,000(2)				
空室率(2%)		▲1,488	▲1,620	1	3bd-1ba	1,300㌦	2,850㌦	3,000㌦
				1	2bd-1ba	1,475㌦	2,000㌦	2,250㌦
				1	1bd-1ba	985㌦	1,350㌦	1,500㌦
合計	45,120	72,912(1)	79,380(2)	3		3,760㌦	6,200㌦	6,750㌦

コメント	ロケーションはB+。賃貸契約は全室月決めのため、購入後2か月通知で賃料値上げ可能。全改装後、売値145万ドルでCAP2.79%(1)、CAP3.25%(2)となり、純利益29.6万㌦見込む。予想賃料、総支出ともにかなり保守的に見積もっている。

補章
物件・案件紹介

物件9

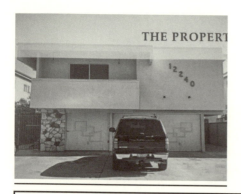

住所：12240 Pacific Avenue, Los Angeles (Mar Vista/Palms), CA 90066

物件内容			運営支出（売却$5.75M推定）	
価格	$ 買4,250,000(売5,750,000)		固定資産税(1.25%)	71,875
戸数	11		保険	4,000
建物面積(s.f., m2)	6,532	600m2	管理費(4%)	10,584 (1) 11,736(2)
土地面積(s.f., m2)	7,499	689m2	AM費	
築年	1964		修理・維持費	3,000
建物比率	25%→70%		電気・ガス・水道・ゴミ	9,000
償却額（4年）	4,025,000㌦ (70%)		各種サービス	8,000
CAP(推定ネット利回り) *	2.65%(1)、3.14%(2)			
年間償却額（$1=110円）1年	1億1,068万円			
1戸当り価格	$ 522,727			
リノベーション費用：			ライセンス	1,500
[内訳] 外側 8.5万㌦、ユニット内：25.82万㌦、その他9万㌦	$ 433,200			
NOI（全改装後）	$ 152,641(1)、180,304(2)		その他	1,000
取得費用（推定）	約 75,000㌦		リザーブ	3,000
総コスト合計 *（推定）	$ 4,900,000 (含販売手数料)		合計（全改装後）	$ 111,959(1) 113,108(2)

収入			各戸内訳			
賃料	270,000 (1)	299,400 (2)	戸数	タイプ	改装後 1	2
空室率(2%)	▲5,400	▲5,988	2	2bd-2ba	2,750㌦	2,850㌦
			7	1bd-1ba	2,000㌦	2,250㌦
			2	0bd-1ba	1,500㌦	1,750㌦
合計	264,600(1)	293,412(2)	11		22,500㌦	24,950㌦

コメント　ロケーションはB+。人気のウエストLAのMar Vista・Palmsエリア。11戸のうち10戸が空室。購入後すぐに改装工事開始可能。全改装後、売値575万ドルでCAP2.65%(1)、CAP3.14%(2)となり、純利益85万㌦見込る。予想賃料、総支出ともに保守的に見積もっている。

補章
物件・案件紹介

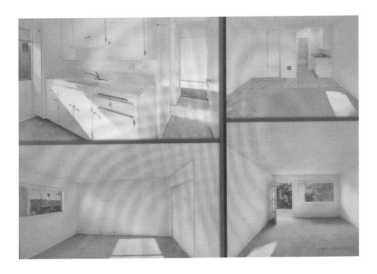

物件10

住所:1322 Amethyst Street, Redondo Beach, CA 90277

物件内容			運営支出(売却$2.5M 推定)	
価格	$	買1,599,000(売2,500,000)	固定資産税(1.25%)	31,250
戸数		4	保険	2,100
建物面積(s.f., m2)	4,365	401m2	管理費($500/mo)	6,000
土地面積(s.f., m2)	5,607	515m2	AM 費	
築年		1963	修理・維持費	1,000
建物比率		64%→75%	電気	659
償却額(4年)		1,875,000ﾄﾞﾙ(75%)	ガス	0
CAP(推定ネット利回り)*		3.09%(1), 3.39%(2)	水道	1,399
年間償却額 ($1=110円)1年		5,156 万円	ゴミ	1,001
1戸当り価格	$	625,000	ランドスケーピング	720
リノベーション費用:				
[内訳] 3Bed:7.5万ﾄﾞﾙ、2Bed: 5万ﾄﾞﾙ x2, 1Bed: 3万ﾄﾞﾙ	$	205,000		
NOI(全改装後)	$	77,208(1), 84,891(2)	その他	1,000
取得費用(推定)		約 25,000ﾄﾞﾙ		
総コスト合計*(推定)	$	1,929,000 (含販売手数料)	合計(全改装後)	$ 45,129

収入				各戸内訳			
賃料	73,800	124,200(1)	132,000(2)	戸数	タイプ 現賃料	改装後1	2
空室率(1.5%)		▲1,863	▲1,980	1	3bd-3ba 2,700ﾄﾞﾙ	3,500ﾄﾞﾙ	3,750ﾄﾞﾙ
				2	2bd-2ba 1,300ﾄﾞﾙ	2,500ﾄﾞﾙ	2,650ﾄﾞﾙ
				1	1bd-1ba 850ﾄﾞﾙ	1,850ﾄﾞﾙ	1,950ﾄﾞﾙ
合計	73,800	122,337(1)	130,020(2)	4	6,150ﾄﾞﾙ	10,350ﾄﾞﾙ	11,000ﾄﾞﾙ

コメント	ロケーションはA-。2ベッドルームはバスが2あるので、高目に賃貸できる。全改装後、売値250万ドルでCAP3.09%(1), CAP3.39%(2)となり、純利益57.1万ﾄﾞﾙ見込む。予想賃料、総支出ともに保守的に想定。

補章
物件・案件紹介

物件11

住所:18306 Grevillea Avenue, Redondo Beach, CA 90278

物件内容			運営支出(売却$1.35M推定)	
価格	$	買 630,000 (売 1,350,000)	固定資産税(1.25%)	16,875
戸数		3	保険	1,800
建物面積(s.f., m2)		2,500 230m2	管理費($450/mo)	5,400
土地面積(s.f., m2)		4,506 414m2	AM費	
築年		1940	修理・維持費	900
建物比率		10%→75%	電気	900
償却額(4年)		1,875,000 ゜,(75%)	ガス	600
CAP(推定ネット利回り) *		2.84%(1), 3.11%(2)	水道	1,200
年間償却額 ($1=110円) 1年		5,156万円	ゴミ	900
1戸当り価格	$	630,000		
リノベーション費用:				
[内訳] 2Bed: 7.5万゜、1Bed: 3万゜x2	$	135,000		
NOI (全改装後)	$	38,390(1), 41,936(2)	その他	1,000
取得費用 (推定)		約 10,000゜.		
総コスト合計* (推定)	$	1,929,000 (含販売手数料)	合計 (全改装後)	$ 29,575

収入			各戸内訳			
賃料	69,000 (1)	72,600 (2)	戸数	タイプ	改装後1	2
空室率(1.5%)	▲1,035	▲1,089	1	2bd-2ba	2,250゜.	2,350゜.
			2	1bd-1ba	1,750゜.	1,850゜.
合計	67,965(1)	71,511(2)	3		5,750゜.	6,050゜.

コメント　ロケーションはB+~A-。本物件は現在一軒家(2LDK)を全面改装し、後ろのガレージに2つ1LDKを追加改装後、売値135万ドルでCAP2.84%(1), CAP3.11%(2)となり、純利益57.9万゜見込む。予想賃料、総支出ともに保守的に想定。

補章
物件・案件紹介

物件12

住所：17412 Queens Lane, Huntington Beach, CA 92648

物件内容			運営支出（売却$1.75M 推定）	
価格	$ 買1,197,500(売1,750,000)		固定資産税(1.25%)	21,875
戸数	4		保険	1,600
建物面積(s.f., m2)	3,430	315m2	管理費($500/mo)	6,000
土地面積(s.f., m2)	6,930	637m2	AM費	
築年	1964		修理・維持費	1,000
建物比率	14%→70%		電気	491
償却額（4年）	1,225,000㌦(70%)		ガス	778
CAP(推定ネット利回り) ＊	3.055%(1), 3.325%(2)		水道	1,658
年間償却額 ($1=110円) 1年	3,368万円		ゴミ	1,554
1戸当り価格	$ 437,500		ランドスケーピング	1,200
リノベーション費用：				
[内訳] 2Bed: 4万㌦ x4	$ 160,000			
NOI（全改装後）	$ 53,468(1), 58,172(2)		その他	1,000
取得費用（推定）	約25,000㌦			
総コスト合計＊（推定）	$ 1,432,500 (含販売手数料)		合計（全改装後）	$ 37,156

収入			各戸内訳				
			戸数	タイプ	現賃料	改装後 1	2
賃料	64,200	88,800(1) 93,600(2)	4	2bd-1ba	1,350㌦	1,850㌦	1,950㌦
空室率(2%)		▲1,776 ▲1,872					
ランドリー		3,600					
合計	64,200	90,624(1) 95,328(2)	4		5,350㌦	7,400㌦	7,800㌦

コメント	ロケーションはB+。レントコントロールはない。購入後2か月通知で賃料値上げ可能。全改装後、売値175万ドルでCAP3.055%(1), CAP3.325%(2)となり、純利益31.75万㌦見込む。予想賃料、総支出とも保守的に見積もり。

あとがき

人生100年時代といわれています。医療技術・設備の発達・進歩、食料・食品の品質向上等などで平均寿命が年々伸びています。もう60歳定年という社会構造・人生設計では対応しきれなくなっています。あと40年ほど人生が残ることになるわけですから、第二の人生の設計をしなければなりません。ひとつの考え方、対応の仕方として、60歳定年になった後も就職すればよい。つまり働き続ければよいと考えられますが、60歳を過ぎて就職することは非常に難しいです。そのためにも何か仕事ができることがあればよいのですが、なかなか難しいと思われます。そのような状態で結論からいえば、不動産投資を自分の事業、ビジネスとしておくことは、先のことを考えれば定年後も収入を確保することができ、安心できます。

また、最近はロボットやAIが発達し、いずれ取って代わられる職も出てくるということで、穏やかではありません。このAIですが、これからどんどん世に出てくると思われていますが、アメリカでは何年も前から利用されています。有名なゴールドマンサックスはこのAIをすでに活用し、2000年に600人いた証券部門のトレーダーを2016

年にはたった2人にまで減らしています。600人がたった2人！ これは本当に驚きです。今後は2人もいなくなって、AIがすべて対応するのでしょう。日本は実はこの点において相当遅れています。このゴールドマンサックスは2000年にすでに導入しているのです。またAIの素晴らしいというか、恐ろしい点は、学習能力があって自分で学習、つまり活用すればするほど、どんどん自分で学習し、データが増えてさらに能力がアップすることです。

これからの世界は、今まで経験したことのないような状況を迎えるといわれています。2040年から2050年ごろから、世界の人口は減少していくといわれています。とくに日本は、スーパー超高齢者社会に突き進んでいます。高齢者がどんどん増えていく一方、若い産業労働人口が減っていきます。その減少する労働人口の代わりに、ロボットやAIがどんどん出てきて、単純作業の代替だけではなく、専門性の高い職業も取って代わるでしょう。すでに銀行では融資業務はロボットとAIに任せる動きになっていくといわれています。将来のことは本当に不安で心配です。職がなくなるかもしれませんから。

自動車も、文字どおり自動運転で自分は運転しなくても大丈夫。最初のうちはロボットやAIが代わって運転すると思いますが、いずれは完全自動運転になるでしょう。ドローンが荷物を運ぶことに利用されるようですが、技術的にはドローン・タクシー、空飛ぶタ

あとがき

クシーができ上がっていて、あとは実用に向けて研究されているそうです。

また、3Dプリンター技術はたいへんなもので、ほとんどのものをコピーというより造り出しています。今やオフィスまで造っています。

このようにいろいろな新しい技術が世に出てきて、周りや社会が一変するのが、すぐそこに来ています。ある統計で使用者5000万人に達するまでの時間が、テレビが13年、インターネットが3年、ツイッターが9ヶ月だそうです。進歩した新しい技術が圧倒的な速さで世に伝わっていきます。どんどん世の中が変わっていくのです。

しかしながら、世の中がどんなに進歩・発展しても、人間の居場所は必要でなくなりません。つまり、不動産は常に必要なのです。ロボットやAIの活躍で仕事がなくなっても、寝る場所は必要です。不動産業界にもAIの利用が考えられ、自分の希望にぴったりの物件をAIが探してくれるというものです。不動産の取引において、AIは十分に活用され

ると思いますし、そのほうが便利でしょう。しかしながら、物件そのものはなくなりません。食事をしたり、お風呂に入ったり、居間でくつろいだり、寝室で寝たり、などなど、人間が生きていく、生活していくためには、不動産物件は必要なんです。

自分を守り、しっかりと収入を得て人生100年時代を乗り切っていくために、不動産投資は最適の事業・ビジネスと考えられます。不動産はこれから日本だけに留まらず、海外、とくにアメリカの西海岸を資産の一部に入れるべきです。アメリカの不動産市況見通しは、序章で述べましたように、明るいし非常に力強く、堅調に推移していくことは確実とみられます。本書をぜひ参考にしていただいてアメリカ不動産投資を成功に導いてください。アメリカ不動産投資が成功することはもちろんのこと、健康で充実した人生を送れますことを祈念致します。

最後になりましたが、本書の出版にご尽力いただきました、プラチナ出版の今井代表取締役社長に謝辞を表したいと思います。

●著者紹介

金井規雄（かない　のりお）

立命館大学経済学部卒、カリフォルニア大学院統計学修士号。
東京三菱UFJ銀行（為替資金および企業融資担当）入行ロスアンジェルス支店勤務後、Bank of the West日本企業部を経て、2004年コスモ・インベストメント(不動産仲介・コンサルティング)を設立、現在に至る。
カリフォルニア州不動産仲介ライセンス、カリフォルニア州保険ライセンス保有。
米国での仲介実績多数。
現地の銀行、会計士、弁護士、保険業者、管理会社などとの幅広いネットワークを持つ。
著書に「安全！確実！アメリカ不動産投資のすべて」「ドル資産を持て！世界最強の通貨によるアメリカ不動産投資戦略」
（いずれも週刊住宅新聞社）がある。

アメリカでの資産形成の問い合わせは、下記アドレスまで
Cosmo Investment
2512 Artesia Blvd.,Suite 250-D,Redondo Beach,CA 90278 USA
https:// www.cosmoinvestusa.com/
E-mail: cosmokanai@gmail.com

アメリカ不動産投資の実態。
在米40年の元バンカーが多数の成功事例を元に実証！

2018年5月22日　初版発行　　Ⓒ2018

著　者　金井規雄
発行人　今井　修
印　刷　モリモト印刷株式会社
発行所　プラチナ出版株式会社
　　　　〒104-0061　東京都中央区銀座1丁目13-1
　　　　ヒューリック銀座一丁目ビル7F
　　　　TEL 03-3561-0200　FAX 03-3562-8821
　　　　http://www.platinum-pub.co.jp
　　　　郵便振替　00170-6-767711（プラチナ出版株式会社）

落丁・乱丁はお取り替えいたします。
ISBN978-4-909357-17-5

プラチナ出版の本

海外不動産投資ならプラチナ出版
好評発売中！

ISBN978-4-909357-03-8
四六判並製・236頁
本体価格　1,500円

アメリカ西海岸で不動産投資
7年で1億円！

金井 規雄 著

ロス在住の元バンカーが"老後破産"しないための秘策
「絶対資産」づくりを提唱!!

最新情報はプラチナ出版公式 WEB サイトから！

https://www.platinum-pub.co.jp/ | 検索 | プラチナ出版